FILLING THE VOID

YOUR GUIDE TO DISCOVERY AND RECOVERY

by
STEVEN T. GINSBURG

Steven T. Ginsburg

ACKNOWLEDGEMENTS

How will I ever get this part right? There are so many, too many to thank...This entire book could be just my acknowledgement of those who have done so much for me. I will do my best.

First and foremost, to my Lord and Savior Jesus Christ: It's by Your grace and mercy that I breathe and have life to write these words.

To my remarkable wife, Nicole: You are the light and love of my life. I will never deserve you but will spend this life living to honor you. Thank you, baby, for being mine. Nicole, you have been a daily source of love and inspiration, and you have been the quintessential epitome of why I have strived to live the passage of Ephesians 5:25: "Husbands, love your wives, just as Christ loved the church and gave himself up for her."

To our beautiful, remarkable children, Brayden Isaiah and Marlia Grace: You are Christ's greatest gift to your mother and me. Boo boos, we love you endlessly, but nowhere near to the degree that Jesus loves you...Because God made you that way.

To Alexis Burns, you are a remarkable mentor, friend, and muse. Thank you for telling me plainly, "Steve, you must do this." Thank you for helping me begin.

To Laurence and Brenda Cohen, my summer parents from age 7 to 18. Eight weeks a year, my childhood years were filled with bliss, self-esteem, love, and empowerment. Thank you for what you gave me and so many others at Camp Maplehurst. Those were precious gifts and continue to contribute to who I am and what I have become. I love and respect you both.

To my parents: my father, Sheldon; my stepmother, Rose; my mother, Joan; and my stepfather, David (may he rest in peace. Proud to make you proud.). To my father-in-law, Gary, and my mother-in-law, Pam (our guardian angel in heaven... oh how we miss you). You all are the ingredients in vast parts of the landscape of my foundation.

To my big brother, Howard, and my big sister, Linda: I love you both. I will always be your baby brother. And to my remarkable niece and nephews Zachary, Max, Matthew, Chase, and Samantha: you are loved beyond measure and you all were my trial run into Fatherhood. I'm so blessed and proud to be your uncle. To my brother-in-law, Carl: Bro, you're my BRO! To my sister-in-law, Kelly: we love you. Please paint more—you're so, so talented.

To our remarkable Pastor Jason Graves and his wife, Pastor Corri Graves: We love you both. We stand grateful for your place in our walk. Jason, a heartfelt thank you for the example you have set as a husband and a father, as well as for your drive and desire to teach and lift any and all up to know the eternal truth. Thank you for being my brother in Christ and my friend.

To our friends, our peeps, our core group, whom we love, adore, live, laugh, eat, do Bible study, raise all our babies, and travel with, as well as to all our other family members who have continued to lift us up in prayer and who have supported this work and our walk: You all know who you are. We could not and would not do this without you all. We love you. We just LOVE you!

For all the men and women who still suffer, as I've suffered.
To this diabolical disease that tells so many they have no disease.
There is an answer. There is a solution. There is hope.
My Heavenly Father showed me this greatest truth
amidst my life of lies.

In gratitude and with a servant's heart, always in His name...

TABLE OF CONTENTS

Steven T. Ginsburg

INTRODUCTION

"This is your last chance. If you don't do something now,
then the last thing your loved ones or children will ever hear is
the sound of your heart monitor going flat."
-Author's Catchphrase

Addiction. There, I said it. No amount of any substance or combination of such can fill *the void*. It beckons you, screams at you, and insists you satisfy it and answer its call. *The void* I carried fed an addiction that demanded everything I had, all the time, and propelled me to a path of complete demise.

It begins with the feeling of emptiness, a *void*, which beckons many of us throughout our lives. The time and money we've pursued to fill that *void* have often proven destructive, and for many, deadly. From 2011–2015, excessive alcohol use was responsible for an annual average of 93,000 deaths. This harrowing statistic is coupled with data regarding years shaved prematurely from alcoholics lives...which equates to 2.7 million years of potential life lost! In 2018, more than 67,000 people lost their lives to drug addiction. That's 5,583 people a month losing their battle to drugs and leaving loved ones with sorrow to carry for the rest of their lives.

Do you recognize a *void* in your life? You know—times where you feel a tremendous gap that just can't be filled. Instead, the gap is plugged with doubts, fears, and words in your mind that ring out and won't subside.

You struggle with self-esteem, never quite hitting the mark, although you know you had so much potential. For many, you continue to live out the self-fulfilled prophecy of these lies. Does any of this sound familiar?

You probably feel alone. **You are not alone**

You are most likely struggling daily with a burden that seems insurmountable. **That is a lie!**

You may feel broken beyond repair, even "terminally unique" (as we say in recovery). **That, too, is false!**

I, and countless others, have wrestled the demon of a *void* and come out on the other side. While trudging through, I learned to practice self-love. **You can, too!**

There is real, tangible courage in owning what owns us. The first step toward any solution is admitting a solution is needed.

So who am I, and why should you listen to me? **I'm a survivor**, someone who made it through and lived to tell about it. More importantly, I am someone who wants to help others gain the same freedom.

I've often described myself as a graduate of the "University of Life." Early on, I enjoyed a long, profitable career in the time-share industry. That being said, no matter how much my career flourished, or how much I earned, I never felt fulfilled. Today, having gained such wisdom and knowledge based on a painful path to a life of fullness and freedom, I hope to help you and others who struggle like I did.

I look forward to sharing this time with you. Thank you for taking that first step to trust the process, allowing me to share my experience in hopes it can help you, too.

Read this book and put in the time to answer the study questions following each chapter. In addition, the highlights— "Rays of Light," if you will—are summary points from what you read and a lead-in to the questions that follow. I believe that approaching each chapter as a weekly exercise will serve you best. Take your time, and truly dive into what fits and where it fits. If you find a section or an area that has you "stuck," step back and pray or meditate on it. I've also included commonly used phrases and quotes at the end of many chapters, a practice reminiscent of what I call "AA Room Talk." Please realize you can always feel free to e-mail directly with any questions. This is an exciting part of the process, and I'm blessed and privileged to have this work serve you and your loved ones.

Apply it. Stick with it all the way to the end. I'm with you every step, and I hope you will join the long list of survivors who have made it to the other side where they experience the peace we all seek when we try through so many other means to fill *the void*.

CHAPTER 1
RESURRECTION

*"We will suddenly realize that God is doing for us
what we could not do for ourselves."*

Alcoholics Anonymous: Promises #12[iv]

November 11, 2004 is an evening I will never forget. The only thing that changed in my life on that day was everything; everything I'd ever known, and everything I had become as a result of all the things I had ever done. People in recovery talk about hitting the bottom, and that was the night I hit mine. The moment that started my downward fall came many years before and will be retold in the pages to come. But this night was the one that would radically transform my sojourn in this world.

I will never forget the darkness. I sat alone in a one-bedroom apartment in Westwood, California. At this point, I kept all the window blinds shut, trying my hardest to block out the rest of the world and not have them see what I had become. I free-based cocaine, which fueled a massive amount of paranoia and delusions driven by fear that people who lived near me, knew me, or knew of me would find out what I was doing and would come to get me. It was a dark place and time in my life, the epitome of being completely alone and starving for anything to just keep me alive. At this point in my disease, I didn't have anyone in my life near me, nor would it have been suitable to have had anyone around.

It felt like sheer terror. The minute I started to use, my heart rate would go up. I heard dark, powerful voices in my head, fueling my fear that the door would be busted down at any moment, and I'd be hauled off to jail. Everything was so twisted outside of reality that I started to feel relieved when I began having seizures because I didn't think I would survive until the next morning. It would all be over, and I wouldn't have to live in this hell any longer.

At that point, I had been ingesting drugs for years, but that night I smoked so much that I began to have episodes in which I would feel like I was falling backward or seeing through distortions and blurred vision. As the darkness overtook me, I could feel the carpet gripped tightly under my fingers while I started to slip away. I was elated and relieved to think the end was near, knowing my death would be that final swoop of revenge and retribution I had long sought to pay back for years of loss and pain. I thought I would not wake up. The pain would be over, the emptiness would subside, the incomprehensible demoralization would vanish, and the anger—that blistering anger—would finally be satiated. This would be the last blackout. It would finally be over.

No one, most of all myself, could have ever imagined what happened next. Somehow, as I slipped quietly toward the mysteries of eternity on the other side, the expected trajectory was altered by the will of a power outside of me and eminently greater than anything in the physical world I was leaving. An undetermined amount of time had passed while I lay unconscious on the floor when suddenly my eyes slid open and snapped into focus on the white ceiling above me, a vision forever imprinted in my memory. In that first moment of my resurrected life, I literally laughed out loud. I found it ironic, remarkable, and preposterous that I was alive! How was it that I had survived the night?

The next moment I remember was transcendent, as though hours or even days of careful thought, prayer, or meditation had been working on me outside the bounds of time. It was arguably the greatest moment of my existence. First, I felt the compulsion to sit up, which I did slowly. I then bent my right leg under the other and rolled over, catching myself with outstretched hands on the floor. From there I easily slid backward onto my feet, clasped my hands together and prayed, *"God, if you will not let me die, please give me my life back in sobriety."*

One would think this remarkable starting point would have been enough to change my life's trajectory, but this simple request set things in motion I could never have imagined as an even greater revelation waited for me. You see, I was raised in a traditional Jewish household in Highland Park,

Illinois—a suburb of Chicago so predominantly Jewish that I would liken it to being raised in Israel.

The area in which I grew up was filled with Jewish families. My friends and I were all raised to go to temple, attend Hebrew school, and to honor all the traditional customs and Jewish holidays. But I always felt I were just going through the motions; I never felt a genuine connection with the Jewish culture. It was all superficial. I did it because it was expected of me. I was even thrown out of Hebrew school, and I didn't care.

My family were more like practicing Jews by obligation, and we were typically in and out of synagogue services in an hour. But even in a barely practicing Jewish household, there were little-to-no references to Christ, the New Testament, or especially the Holy Spirit.

Yet in my darkest hour, I cried out to Jesus. Somehow, without any preparation or real understanding, I knew Christ had the power to heal me and change me. I wanted that then more than ever.

Even though I was raised Jewish, I knew about Jesus because of key people who were placed in my life. These people showed something so powerful through their words and actions toward me—they lived out His love by demonstrating it to me. I received it, even though I didn't understand it. It was there all along, tucked inside of me, waiting for me to reach for Him when I crashed to my bottom. I had only one person to call upon because there was no other answer. So I knew Jesus Christ was God. That's all I knew, but on the morning of November 12, I woke up, I prayed, and I called out to Him to save me. In my belief, He saved me. I knew it, and it was done.

You see, it was with an absolute resolve of my heart and belief that I asked Him to enter my life and take over completely. As the thoughts formed, even before they tumbled from my mouth in prayer, the death grip of that *void* which had engulfed and devoured my young life so far had been irreparably compromised.

Now, all I had to do was follow the light out of the darkness.

Rays of Light—Resurrection:

The Lord is, was, and always will be present.

Each phase of our journey is redeemed by Him for the glory of His kingdom.

The deepest, darkest valley is an open door for liberation and fulfillment to enter into a miracle beyond anything we have ever imagined. He loves us that much....

STUDY 1:
RESURRECTION

Introduction:

In a moment or moments of utter despair, we may find a birth of hope beyond any expectation or rescue we could imagine. Many of us who share these thoughts have had such moments. This offers an opportunity for inventory and reflection. There are landmarks, "God Shots," reminders, and flat-out pure-proving points that will show us action is a must, especially when we stare down a true "darkest before the dawn" moment.

Faith without works *is* dead (James 2). Some of the most monumental achievements by achievers have been at the time or times where all seemed lost and insurmountable. These times are never the end, nor are they failures. They are the beginnings of a triumph waiting to take shape.

Here are a few familiar names of people who have faced similar issues to the ones I've described and emerged on the other side: Robert Downey, Jr., Sir Elton John, Bradley Cooper, Drew Barrymore, Keith Urban, and Jamie Lee Curtis. Their methods may have been different, as all of our walks are unique. But the similarities, not the differences, are what weave the fabrics of those who have survived the darkness together. Let's get started!

Step 1: Create your list.

Now is the time to begin toward triumph on the other side by taking clear and decisive action where the ties that have bound you are concerned. You may use the space below or start a companion journal to list an honest inventory of what ails you. What are your addictions, your weaknesses, and your actions that contribute to your addiction? There is no wrong answer here. Don't rush through this first step. This is the time for you to be honest with yourself and list your inventory of what ails you.

_____

_____

_____

_____

_____

_____

_____

_____

_____

_____

_____

_____

Step 2: What's the answer?

Taking your list from Step 1 above—out to the side of each item you listed—put what you feel could be the solution to each item. There are no wrong answers. This is an important step—search deep inside yourself to find what you truly believe are the solutions. These may change through the course of this study, but today's list provides you an opportunity to look back to where you started and see how far this journey has taken you.

Encouragement and Wisdom:

Throughout each study I will refer to the Bible verses and the wisdom from which helped me take each step toward healing while on my journey. I encourage you to slowly read aloud each of the verses, and personalize them as if they were directly including you in their meaning. (For example, for the verse below, read out loud, "*I* was taught…".)

"You were taught, with regard to your former way of life, to put off your old self, which is being corrupted by its deceitful desires; to be made new in the attitude of your minds; and to put on the new self, created to be like God in true righteousness and holiness." Ephesians 4:22-24

Want to go one step more? Memorize this verse and repeat it over each day. It's here to encourage you!

Step 3: Let's reflect.

Prayer is one of the key foundational blocks I used in my recovery journey. Prayer offers you a chance to have a safe one-on-one conversation with someone who will always listen and care for you through each stage of your recovery. I can't express enough the importance of the exercise of prayer and speaking your heart out loud. This is essential for maintaining your recovery and to have each day build upon the other, which only comes through daily conversation with God. Never be ashamed or hesitant to seek the help you need. There is always an answer, always a solution, always a better way.

Take as long as you need, start talking, and don't worry about how you say what is on your heart. The important thing to remember is that God is always there for you—twenty-four/seven—and you can't say anything wrong to Him. Just start praying.

Last Step: Send yourself a note to remember today.

Give yourself the gift of recording how you see who you are today and how this turning point in your life will change who you are going forward. In the space below, write a summary of what led you to reading this book including details and key players to the event that brought you to this turning point. This may well be an issue in your life that has been resolved, is resolved, or needs to be liberated with the gift of resolution. I've left room for a couple of healthy paragraphs, but feel free to go to a journal or extra paper if need be.

My note of encouragement to you:

During the next thirty days, take part in your very own committed prayer cycle. Be intentional about this. Choose a consistent time and place to do this every day. Make this your commitment to a long-standing must-have in your life. Decide what you want to see the Lord do *with you* and *for you* where this area is concerned. Ask Him this as part of your prayer time.

Over the next thirty days, when you rise and when you prepare to end your day, earnestly ask for the Lord's will to prevail over your life and for his presence, love, and light to relieve you of this burden of addiction. Stay with it. You are worth it, and God is present. The best is yet to come.

CHAPTER 2
CREATION OF
THE VOID

"We will not regret the past nor wish to shut the door on it."

Alcoholics Anonymous: Promise #3[vi]

Life is a succession of moments joined into days, seasons, and years. Like a signpost on a long road, some moments stand out and are preserved forever in my memory, while most others fade away as life progresses. We don't exactly know why, but some memories, such as was one of my first detailed below, mark a dramatic change of direction.

I remember it was very dark. The physical sensation comes back to me even as I recall this moment. My mother stood at the top of our stairs saying something to my father who was standing at the bottom. All I could understand from her words was that my dad was leaving, and everything in my world was about to change. My parents would divorce because my father had been unfaithful in the marriage.

I was four years old. I don't have many memories that forewarned me of the impact this moment would have on me. I didn't see the divorce coming. The shock of watching it unfold in front of me at such a young age became the catalyst that started me down the road of *the void*.

Looking back, the only other warning sign I remember was a comment my mom made to my dad in surprise when he announced we were taking a family trip to Wisconsin. My mom said she thought the trip was for the two of them to "help find their way". I was aware of that conversation, even though I don't think I should have been. It's like you instinctively know something is wrong, but you dismiss it in the moment to keep the peace.

That incident with my parents and remembering them at the stairs still physically affects me today. Despair and pain grabbed me during this event. That was where all this started. That *void*, that emptiness, was my open wound and a scar on my life. It was a road sign that never faded, and it marked a noticeable shift in where I went, who I became, and why I ended up on this journey.

I remember an uneasiness took hold of me and swelled into a sense of tangible and concrete duress in my four-year-old body. The realization that my dad was leaving filled my heart with desperation. I felt powerless to stop him—and I was torn. This was the beginning of *the void* that would stay with me for many more years, an emptiness I carried and sought to fill, a driving force behind so many of the trials and tribulations to come.

My father, a self-made man, worked hard to build a lucrative and successful business, but his once-a-week visits after the divorce could not provide the emotional stability I so desperately needed. Nor could this short amount of time replace the balance I had known seeing him every day when he returned home from his work.

To compound this impact, he eventually remarried a lady who was verbally and psychologically abusive; she had no desire for children, especially those who were not her own. This "wonderful" (sarcasm noted) participant on my journey was a towering woman named Kathleen. She had a sharp tongue and a short fuse, which eventually caused her to become my father's second ex-wife.

Kathleen had no time or use for a five-year-old who was navigating unchartered waters. She was cruel and took delight in other's discomforts. Kathleen remained a fixture in my childhood for almost nine years. Eventually, she and my father divorced (a blessing, really), but she had plenty of times and occasions to contribute to the damage that comprised the ingredients of my *void*.

The times I could be with my dad were almost always tainted and spoiled by Kathleen. But there was a light at the end of the tunnel for this chapter in our lives in the form of a woman who entered after the perfect storm of Kathleen had passed. Her name was Rosemarie, and she had worked at my dad's office for several years.

I remember when I first was introduced to Rosemarie, whom I call Rose. I had gone with my dad to his office, and I was eight years old. My father, to a fault, was all about his work—and when he would take me to his office, he was looking for me to be supervised while he worked. This was no "Career Day with Dad" at his office like most children experience. I was delegated to Rose, one of his assistants, and I ended up spending a lot of time with her when I went.

Rose quickly became a solid parental figure in my life. She leaned into me and invested in me. We talked about everything. I didn't know it at the time, but she could genuinely understand what I was going through. She had compassion for me and took me under her wing. It was a lasting friendship, and she was a safe harbor for me when I needed one most.

On the joyful occasions when I would visit my dad at his office, I was glued to Rose's side. Despite having her daily responsibilities with her job, she took care of me entirely during those visits. There were frequent conversations and visits to the office vending machines to get my favorite candy pinwheels. Rose recognized the hurt in me, and I felt safe to tell her anything I was going through. Rose had similar pain in her past—her parents had divorced, as well.

She also saw my humor and wit. We quickly bonded, and she often followed up with my dad to see if "Stevie" (she still calls me this) would be coming for a visit. One thing that I had no awareness of back then was that Rose loved the Lord. I also was unaware that very quickly upon meeting me, she prayed that someday I would come to know Jesus and be saved. This fact would not hold the proper magnitude until later in my life when I hit my bottom through my addiction.

Eventually, Rose and my father, amongst other common interests (me being a major one), fell in love and married. Rose has and does play a critical part in my life as a parent, a friend, and a great spiritual mentor. I will share one of those most pivotal moments in the chapters to come, but Christ's fingerprints were and are all over Rose's place in my life. On the other hand, my mother, Joan, struggled to find her footing as a single parent of three children with specific and significant needs.

I love my mother, but being a single, divorced mom, holding down a new job at a bookstore, and managing a home we couldn't afford with child support payments overwhelmed her. She was hurt, confused, and looking to self-help her way through all the challenges she faced—and that wasn't safe for me.

As a broken family unit, we all needed triage, and we didn't have the right people to help us navigate the choppy waters we were in, yet the waves kept coming. To compound the issue, my mom had three hurt children who lashed out in different ways that challenged her and created instability. It was like the stable adults in my home were replaced with inexperienced parents who only could give us half the time we needed with each one of them. What I inherited going forward was a mix of them treating me like their therapist while also jumping into other relationships that I got dragged into unwillingly. This nightmare came with additional layers of scars in my life that fast-tracked me further into depression and low self-esteem.

My two older siblings handled the divorce from two different extremes. Being so young, these were impressionable years for me, and I didn't know who to follow or what I could trust. My sister was older and well-adjusted. She went on with her life, and the divorce didn't seem to affect her. At least, she never showed that it did.

My brother, on the other hand, took it hard. He was a young teenager, and being the male figure in the home, he felt like he needed to step in and parent me after my father was asked to leave. I saw him carry an enormous pressure of responsibility that he wasn't necessarily asked to carry. He showed his pain through a variety of outbursts. There were times where he and my Mother would have tremendous conflicts as he tried to bear the burden of taking care of our family at such a young age.

Later on my counselor conveyed to me that much of what I witnessed in our household dynamics were disruptive and abusive in the fact that I never truly felt safe. It was a war zone that destroyed everyone in its path, and my family was the casualty.

Looking back now, I simply did not have enough emotional footing in place to allow me to adapt to what I was feeling and experiencing. For me, this was a time of crisis and chaos when the stability I needed was ripped away.

As my childhood progressed, the size and darkness of this *void* only grew through other events, which on the outside, may seem like natural occurrences for a kid. For instance, in primary school, there was the searing shame of being picked last for a team, an unsympathetic spotlight which illuminated my lack of value and provided great ammunition for ridicule. This erosion of social standing made me an easy target for the bullies, who were probably looking for some relief from the same pain I was feeling.

Very early on I was diagnosed with dyslexia, and the constant going in and out of classes for "special education" helped to solidify the divide between me and my peers in the very affluent suburb where I was raised. I can still vividly recall being chastised by my classmates for my inability to learn, to fit in, and for being from a broken household. I felt like a snowball rolling down a hill, taking everything in its path, as it grew bigger and bigger with each part of my life compounding my problems.

Their cruelties fed the monster that would incrementally devour me, showing itself more powerful than me over time and fueling a message I was worthless. As I floundered, sometimes my behavior and conduct were so out of control that the consequences I received would isolate me even more from my peers. This often led to me being excluded from activities with them. This also contributed to a consistent amount of friends and or friends families who no longer wanted to spend time with me if we actually did do something together. This world of isolation that was becoming my reality produced a physical feeling of pain that accompanied all of this. *The void* now had a voice inside of me, and I was a prisoner to it, not strong enough to break away. **I felt like a complete misfit and utterly alone.**

I remember a defining moment shared with my mother that first year after the divorce. I was sitting on the floor in our hallway, and she asked if I wanted to take a bath. I remember putting my back against the wall where I sat and inexplicably cried. I recall my mom, empathetically , saying she wanted to take me to see someone who could help. This conversation would lead to a youth filled with therapy and counselors, all who did their best to help me, but none could provide what I needed to fill that aching emptiness of my soul.

While I was out seeing therapists, at home my mother and brother continued to have confrontations with one another—some of which escalated to physical violence. There was simply no peace in my life, anywhere. Layers of resentment and rage built up and seeped into my being. It wasn't long before I started lashing out. At this point, I was cognizant of my despair, a very real feeling I could not escape. As it continued to grow like a dark cloud that hovered over me, it brought utter hopelessness and loneliness beyond words.

There are more details I could share, but the overview conveys enough to show the inception of emptiness that I would desperately try to fill in the years to come. No one could have ever made me—a hopeless, wounded child—understand then that these trials and tribulations would play a major role in my journey, that they would serve as a catalyst to finding true healing and finally filling that *void* through knowing the Father, the king of heaven.

Now, as an adult, my heart breaks for the young me. If I could, I would hold that boy so close and tell him the truth. I would tell him what only time and experience has taught me. "Hang in there, baby," I would say to that version of myself. "None of this makes sense now, but you are being prepared for something so much bigger, something that will help others." I can feel heavy tears beckon just writing these words.

Never leave before the miracle.

Rays of Light—Creation of the Void:

The trajectory to a destination is dictated by the adversity found along the way.

Our circumstances will one day empower us, through Him, to love and serve one another in the greatest manner imaginable.

Pain in life is inescapable, but endless suffering is optional.

STUDY 2:
CREATION OF
THE VOID

Introduction:

Our history is the foundation of who we are and also serves
as the narrative to who we have and will become. In addition,
the people in our past and present contribute to so much of
what we have done and will do. Our history and the influential
people in it got us to where we are, but they do not have to
control where we're going.

To put a face on what has contributed to our behavior, we
need to look first at the close circle of people around us. Many
of us have relevant parties or people we love dearly who have
played their parts, good and bad, in shaping us into who we
are. They willingly or unwillingly have been what brought us
to where we are with our addictions.

Today, let's go a little deeper in building off what you
accomplished in the first step of *Resurrection* and identify the
people who may have contributed to your addiction.

Step 1: Who are they?

Take a moment and identify the top three people you believe have contributed to where you have arrived. These are the three people who have made the greatest contribution to your gain or to your detriment in leading you to where you are. This list may well change as time moves on.

1._____

2._____

3._____

Step 2: I remember when...

We have all dealt with circumstances that stand out in our minds. These include moments, episodes, and encounters that, much to our joy or dismay, will not dissipate or disappear from our memories.

These moments or experiences stand out as the catalysts in our lives. They molded us and shaped us into who we are. We're looking to create new catalysts going forward— so identifying these from the past helps let them go. We heal because we learn to know how events like these create outcomes we don't desire.

Take as much time as needed and describe three formative moments that stand out and have contributed to the very fabric of who you have become and are becoming in as much detail as you can remember. If you need more space, record this in your journal or on separate paper as needed.

1._____

2._____

3._____

Step 3: Where's the connection?

Looking back now on these people and events, how do they relate to one another? Where and what is the connection between these people and experiences in your life?

Explain:

_____

_____

_____

_____

_____

_____

Step 4: What would you say?

Where the individuals mentioned are concerned, what would you want to share with each of them? What would you want to resolve with each of them? What would you want to acknowledge or affirm with each of them?

1._____

2._____

3._____

Step 5: What would you do differently?

Where your three experiences are concerned, what are you doing today to ensure the good in each of them is preserved? What are you doing today to resolve the turmoil or resentment in each of them?

1._____

2._____

3._____

Encouragement and Wisdom:

"The Lord gives strength to his people; the Lord blesses his people with peace…." Psalm 29:11

"Keep me safe, Lord, from the hands of the wicked; protect me from the violent, who devise ways to trip my feet." Psalm 140:4

"My God is my rock, in whom I take refuge, my shield and the horn of my salvation. He is my stronghold, my refuge and my savior - from violent people you save me. I called the Lord, who is worthy of praise, and have been saved from my enemies." 2 Samuel 22:3-4

Last Step: Let's reflect.

We covered a lot in this session. Please dive into the above and take time to pray. Journal your thoughts where these critical events or people are concerned.

My note of encouragement to you:

The answers, the joy, and the beauty of our journey are in those we have encountered and who have been put in our paths. We should not live in a state of regret where our past is concerned, nor should we forget it, nor are we destined to repeat it. Resentment is the number one offender we must let go of, and we can start by extending grace to those who have hurt us. The thing is…someone most likely hurt them. We will often find the people we have resentment toward were treated much the same way as they treated us. We are all here to grow, give grace, learn, and love as we live together.

The strongest thing you can say to any
who have hurt you is, I forgive you.

Lead different than you have followed.
You intend to help everyone in your influence
to arrive at a much better place.

CHAPTER 3
ADDICTION, THE FALSE MESSIAH

"We are going to know a new freedom and a new happiness."
Alcoholics Anonymous: Promise #2[vii]

When I was fifteen years old, I found it. The healing elixir I had been seeking through all the years of my young life was now put in front of me. At that moment, the first moment I experienced being "high," I was done. Many people who recall their first experience with marijuana will often describe it as "not working" or having little-to-no effect. My circumstances were the complete opposite. After ingesting it just once, I knew marijuana was what I had been missing all along. That gnawing emptiness where I had no answer subsided, and I was catapulted into a realm I had absolutely no idea existed. Suddenly, nothing but uncontrollable—literally, completely uncontrollable—joy, glee, and giddiness filled my emptiness on the inside. I was categorically addicted from the first moment. I simply wanted to feel that way all the time, and now that I had found it, I would not let it go. For the first time I could remember, I was free from the darkness that ruled over me with its cruel power, and by my summation, the glorious light now soothing my weary soul was to be had by smoking pot.

I do not regret any of the circumstances of my first fifteen years on this planet which led me to this moment, as this was where my destiny and God's plan for my life came together. Very simply, it could be no other way. There is a phrase in the world of recovery that is the epitome of my reality at that time:

"Addiction is the solution, not the problem."

Though true, it would be many more years before I could see the addiction I had just entered through the portal of marijuana as my solution, since what followed was an even darker prison of lies, deception, and heartache in greater proportion to what I already knew. For the rest of my life on earth, I will suffer from a progressive illness that began from that very first use, yet in that moment, I dove in headfirst with a smile on my face.

From this starting point until I was nineteen, my addiction grew, magnified, expanded, and eventually overtook me. There were countless occasions when I questioned my use patterns. I would fantasize about not needing to get high. I would visualize myself as stable, productive, strong, and vital, free of "having" to use drugs. The irony was that many of these realities I would dream about occurred while I was heavily under the influence of what I was using. In other words, I was high as a kite and dreaming of a life of sobriety. I was hopelessly addicted to marijuana and needed to ingest it all day and night, along with occasional times when alcohol or other substances would be incorporated.

After graduating high school in Illinois, I went to college in Arizona. At the time, I didn't realize how serious my addiction had become or that I even had a problem. I was out on my own for the first time with cash in my pocket, a new apartment, and a car my father purchased for me.

In the first few weeks of being at college, my problem came out in full force, and I recognized for the first time, I was out of control. At the point of attempting my freshman year in college, I had hit what would be my first bottom.

I found a wonderful and intuitive therapist named Judy, who will always be my guardian angel. She passed away years ago, but I have no doubt she was sent my way to confront me with what I needed to hear—my truth. During our first counseling session, as she heard about my patterns and history, Judy firmly suggested I was an addict and needed in-patient treatment. I thought this premise was preposterous. People who grew up in my community didn't "go to treatment."

I told her I didn't understand why I had to be admitted into in-patient treatment, explaining that I thought regular therapy with her would arrest this condition, as I had been in and out of therapy most of my entire life. She adamantly disagreed, but, thankfully, agreed to see me since I was comfortable with that form of treatment.

In less than a year after our first meeting, Judy's prophetic words became a reality. I was not yet twenty years old, but I looked like death warmed over. I hadn't seen Judy in about four-plus months as I kept making excuses for not keeping up with my visits. The perils of addiction drew me further and further away from the productive work we had embarked upon in her safe home office. When I showed up at her door, I could only be described as in an utterly ravaged condition. I will never forget the look in Judy's eyes when she first saw me. She gasped when she opened the door. Immediately she understood the critical place I had progressed to and shared that she was fearful for my life. We got settled in her office, and I admitted for the first time, although it would not be the last time, that I needed help. The fitting part of what occurred next is that she called my father.

Flash back to months before this pivotal moment in my journey. I had traveled home to Highland Park, Illinois, for Thanksgiving. I managed to pull my Dad aside alone and plainly told him my story. My family didn't know I had dropped out of school or that I was in terrible shape, spiraling toward oblivion. I desperately needed help yet had failed to tell anyone who cared about me. I was doing such a terrific job not showing anyone even remotely close to me the reality of my circumstances. But I couldn't hide from everyone forever. I especially felt the reality of my condition could not be kept from my father, whom I have always considered being brilliant in so many ways. Inevitably I would have to at least tell him something about what was going on in my life before he found out some other way.

For some reason I wasn't expecting what came next. It didn't take long for him to answer my foxhole confession. When he did, he explained to me that the plane ticket back to Arizona was now all that I had, period. My strong, self-made, and successful father made it clear to me that nothing else would be provided any longer. "Get on that flight, find work, and move on with your life" could pretty well sum up what he had to say about my sorry circumstances. This shocked me and should have been my wake-up call. I was in no condition to receive or assimilate his tough love boundaries and lack of enablement.

From the time I was fifteen and started using, up until these events, I had wreaked havoc, failed on a monumental scale, and broken trust after trust in ways that would harden the heart of any parent or loved one. Without understanding the source, my family had been seeing firsthand, blow-by-blow, how my addiction was destroying me.

While I sat there in the counselor's chair waiting for her to call this indomitable father of mine, I was fully aware that this fork in the road hadn't been reached simply because I fell out of bed one day. Rather, the road that brought me there had been steadily constructed piece-by-piece right under my feet from the very first time I used marijuana, which had advanced into the grip of progressively stronger drugs, then on to more reckless behavior and actions as time went by. The emptiness that defined my life and spurred me blindly forward seemed to welcome the wretchedness of this journey, gorging itself on false hope and the bondage of cruel slavery in which I was now dying.

As mentioned earlier, my dad is a pragmatic, self-made man. His initial reaction to Judy's call, based on my history, was that I would have to manage my circumstances and figure it out. Looking back, I fully support and understand my father's reaction. Thankfully, the Lord saw fit to have a wonderful advocate in my corner. I remember Judy spoke boldly to my father about the dire nature of my situation. Simply and precisely, she explained that if I weren't able to get help, the next conversation would be the one he and she would have at my funeral.

As a father today, I try to imagine what my dad must have been going through during that time when the information was conveyed in such a direct and dramatic fashion. I have always seen him as a brilliant man, and I wonder what his internal debate and dialogue must have been as he reckoned with the pending circumstances contingent on his willingness or lack thereof to help me get better. I believe there was an element of divine intervention as he grappled with the situation. I had to have his help and support to get the help I needed. Yet, intrinsically, I hadn't done one single thing to warrant such support. The Lord was present, and He moved on my father's heart. Thirty minutes later, my dad called back and told Judy that whatever it took or wherever I needed to go, to get me there.

These are some of the most revealing and critical milestones of this journey. I see and hear them so clearly now, that they might as well have happened just moments ago. These moments are also foundational pieces and prove to me that my Heavenly Father was guiding and guarding my walk. He has had a plan for me since I was knitted in my mother's womb. These incidents and circumstances, although trying and difficult, were not for my demise. They were realized for the glory of His kingdom at what I was ultimately called to do with my life. My salvation was the reason I was on this journey, and for me, that was non-negotiable. There simply could be no other way. The blessing is what hope was provided through the gift of His mercy and grace on my life.

Today, as I write these words, I see how the Lord was present at that moment, and that when I needed a mountain to be moved, He moved on my father's heart.

Rays of Light—Addiction: The False Messiah

The emptiness in all of us beckons and must be satisfied.

No element, substance, or thing can fill the person who cries out.

Conditions in life will dictate the terms. Then choices, both good and bad, will be in response to these unchosen factors.

Everything happens because of something, and no "random" incident is without intention.

STUDY 3:
ADDICTION,
A FALSE MESSIAH

(The real truth of your weakness.)

Introduction:

Coming to terms that we all have weaknesses playing into our insecurities is an important part of understanding why we do what we do. Our past is filled and influenced by the people and events in our lives. However, they don't control us going forward. They don't lead us—they each simply are what they are—a weakness. Once we identify these weaknesses, we can become stronger in knowing why we have given in to them in the past.

Resentment and comparison to others are some of the many offenders that can show up and potentially cost us everything. The ongoing battle in our head is the knowledge that we suffer from a disease, while the disease itself wants us to believe that it does not exist. This divisive mindset is a tool that the enemy wants to use against us.

I want you to think of yourself as wearing a suit of armor like you would picture a knight wearing. The suit is your protection against anything that wants to attack. At this point your armor probably looks like mine, full of scuffs or chinks that we carry as addicts—traits common to us all. We bring these on by the obstacles we face and overcome, leaving their marks on our armor. These are reminders to keep ourselves safe and to safeguard what matters most in our spiritual and physical well-being.

They are not random or accidental. They were bred and born from our pain and our past; they took root to take hold of us. However, what was meant to destroy us is what will, in fact, give us strength to continue. Our experiences become our gifts if we look at how they teach us or bridle our steps. I like to call these "bricks of tragedy" that can build our impenetrable fortress against the disease—a stronghold that will give us a safe place to triumph as we learn step by step, day by day, to tame the beast. Then our attention can change from survival to what we do outwardly to give back and put others first.

We keep it all by giving it away, and this journey is one of awareness, humility, and selflessness.

"For many are invited, but few are chosen." Matthew 22:14

Step 1: What seems stronger than you?

If we step back and are honest with ourselves, we can identify the things in our lives we have a hard time saying no to. Back in our first study, I had you identify what ails you. Take a moment and read what you wrote again. Out of your list, can you narrow down what you feel are the top three things you would struggle to say no to? List those here.

1._____

2._____

3._____

Step 2: Are they really that strong?

Superman was made powerless by kryptonite in the comic book series. His enemies would use this to take him down, even though he was the strongest man in the universe. But God didn't create us that way. He created us with the assurance that nothing was greater than what He created us to be, and that God was in control of all things. This means that God is in control of the things you listed above and is definitely stronger than them.

Knowing that Superman's weakness was just fiction, and there isn't really anything that has power or control over you, let's revisit what you wrote above and write out what you can do to avoid these in your life. Consider this your strengthening time... time to allow you to grow, get stronger, and trust that God will change this in your life. That's His promise.

Here, list three ways you can avoid your kryptonite:

1._____

2._____

3._____

Step 3: Put together your support team.

We all struggle to do anything on our own—especially when that involves change or facing anything we have allowed to become stronger than us. Perhaps it's associated with fears or temptations that we have allowed into our lives that feed destructive habits.

Be encouraged. You are creating new steps of strength and freedom. These larger-than-life things are powerless in the eyes of God and His will for you. Focus on Him, but also surround yourself with people who support you and understand your goals.

List three people you can surround yourself with who are safe to call on if any temptation or area you listed above (your kryptonite) lands in your path. Then, reach out to them.

My safe people are:

1._____

2._____

3._____

Please note: Help these people know how they can best help you during this transition time. You will get stronger. Your support team will soon become your cheerleaders as they celebrate your recovery milestones with you. But help them understand what you're facing and where you need help. If you call, tell them what you want them to do. Any and all setup time with them will help you know you have someone in your corner. I also encourage you to have prayer with these folks so they can support you through prayer when they aren't on call.

Encouragement and Wisdom:

"No temptation has overtaken you except what is common to mankind. And God is faithful; he will not let you be tempted beyond what you can bear. But when you are tempted, he will also provide a way out so that you can endure it." 1 Corinthians 10:13

"So do not fear, for I am with you; do not be dismayed, for I am your God. I will strengthen you and help you; I will uphold you with my righteous right hand." Isaiah 41:10

"Discretion will protect you, and understanding will guard you." Proverbs 2:11

Last Step: Let's reflect.

We covered a lot in this session. Please dive into the above and take time to pray. Journal where these things have had power over you in the past. Pray specifically that they be removed from your life and ask God to protect you and those around you from them. His promise is that nothing can remove you from his protection—only you can allow yourself to fall. God's strength is enough for all of us.

My note of encouragement to you:

People, places, and things... the "Who's Who List" of natural-born derailments. Take heart. It's an ongoing process, and a beautiful and fulfilling one at that. The cognizant realization of all that surrounds and becomes you is priceless. These factors ultimately will serve you best as you develop, grow, and transcend your day-to-day burdens. A ship in a harbor is safe, but that's not what ships are made for.

CHAPTER 4
RECOVERY IN
THE MEADOWS

*"If we are painstaking about this phase of our development,
we will be amazed before we are halfway through."*

Alcoholics Anonymous: Promises #1[viii]

The facility that was chosen for me, The Meadows, was in Wickenburg, Arizona. When my therapist initially reached out to them, a bed was not available. As I left her office, she begged me to be careful and to be patient, assuring me that a bed would open up, and things would work out. In retrospect, I realize how dire my circumstances were. Judy held a valid fear for my life and well-being as she was worried I would do myself in before I reached the impending safety of treatment.

That night was the first time in my life that I can remember praying. I didn't know the Lord then, but He certainly knew me. I pictured Him close by, always there with me while I squeezed my eyes tight and begged for a bed to open up. Describing this moment reminds me of a story that has always been a part of my life where my recovery is concerned. In this tale, a man who had struggled through many trials and tribulations questions why the Lord wasn't present during his most treacherous times. He's shown in the reflection of his life that in fact those very times were when the Lord was closest and safeguarding him.

I love this word picture because it perfectly describes one of my lowest and saddest moments, on my knees in the bathtub, begging a God I could not see or understand to save my life. What felt to me like a probable tragic ending, was a moment that my very present, loving Heavenly Father had been eagerly waiting all along.

The next morning, my therapist called and relayed the wonderful news that a bed had opened up for me. At the time, it did not dawn on me that the simple reality of "prayer works" was being boldly illustrated for future reference. Plans were made for my older brother to drive me up north to Arizona for treatment the next day. I'll never forget that drive. I was terrified, hopeful, and relieved all at once. I am still cognizant of details about the ride, like the (normally) insignificant song that played on the radio, although the entire evening before, until the last moment when my brother came to pick me up, I was using drugs relentlessly. At some point along the drive I had the thought, "I'm not going to die" Then I said it out loud again and again and again. "I'm not going to die!" It was the cry of someone lost for a long time in a deep cave, who one day sees a pinhole of light shining in the distance.

Along with the memory of that song and the thoughts in my head, I will literally never forget anything about my time at The Meadows. The moment I arrived, I was subjected to one of the first facets of "in-take," a medical assessment and physical examination. I vividly recall streams of tears pouring down my face, which prompted a nurse to ask me, "Are you scared?" I told her I was, but also relieved because I was just so, so tired. This was the beginning of my freedom from the prison that had lured me in with promises to fill the dark *void* in my soul. Through the work done by the remarkable people I met there, both staff and fellow patients, I would come to understand clearly for the first time who I really was and what that meant.

The next step was a very stringent and well-thought-out personality assessment test that took two days to complete. The results and understanding it gave to the staff were utilized for treatment prescriptions and assessment in the weeks to come. My results conclusively identified a massive degree of depression and the highest score possible affirming addictive and alcoholic tendencies and behaviors. This was a shocking reality to face at nineteen years of age—that I had not simply made mistakes in my use of addictive substances, but I was, intrinsically, an addict and an alcoholic.

I spent forty-two days there, and although it was twenty-nine years ago, I remember the time as though it were yesterday. I was one of the youngest people to go through in-patient treatment at The Meadows. They provided me with a design for living and a collection of critical components that shape who I am to this very day.

This was a very special place and a significant time for me in my journey. It was one of the most formative times in my life. From the moment I got there, I inherently knew I was safe, and for the first time I had hope that everything would finally be okay. So much so that I just cried and cried. It was like those people who get stranded on a deserted island with no hope for escape, and then one day a ship arrives. Hope—tangible steps in the right direction where no hope had been.

When a patient first arrives, they put them in a blue jacket so everyone knows they're a newcomer. That way, other patients and staff can lean in to offer added support during those crucial first steps.

Because you stay at the facility, the medical staff is with you twenty-four/seven, and you see the doctor regularly until they know you are stabilized. I remember the staff asking me through those first days repeatedly, "Are you ok?" Although I was so young, I would tell them, "I am just really relieved and happy to be here." I had failed at trying to fix this on my own and finally had the help I needed.

When I had tried to beat my disease before, I didn't understand what or where it came from and why I felt the way I did. This time, the difference came immediately. They tested me with tons of questions, interviews, and assessments that helped to unpack what I had experienced and how I had attempted to cope.

My counselor, who led my group through step-by-step treatment, sat me down and gave me the results of all their assessment tests. I'll never forget her words: "Steven, you score undeniably in the realm of addiction and alcoholism. You have those inherent traits and characteristics that came out over and over to support that your disease is real."

For the first time—the what, why, and how I ended up here were starting to make sense. It clicked! Even from the first time I used, it seemed to drive me. It was more of an obsessive nature, and I knew nothing about recovery, treatment, or a twelve-step program.

Over the next few days, they went over with me the magnitude of what was wrong and convinced me of what I suffered from so they could start taking me in baby steps toward a solution.

I will never forget my counselor, Lane Crawford, who was so firm and transparent about how very high the stakes were for me. Lane honestly cared for me, but would never coddle me nor allow me to manipulate the circumstances. She also held my family accountable for their part and made it clear to them I was fighting for my life.

Ultimately, as a priceless advocate and hero, she left me with a gift that will stay with me always. She explained to me that now that I had stepped out and gotten help and therefore breaking the lineage and chain of dysfunction in my family, I was no longer the broken one, but had become the its strongest member. She was deliberate in conveying this information to me and reiterated it several times. She explained that going forward, because of my passionate and authentic desire to arrest my condition, my family would "go as I would go." This meant that change in my dysfunctional family began with me.

For the first time, I took control to lead my family in a new direction versus destroying them through my behavior they influenced over my past. For many families, if no one has come to the point and place where I did, the vicious cycle continues.

This was a shift in thinking for me. It gave me strength and determination to see it through. I remember her affirming me, "You are now the leader of your family. You have bravely stepped out of your former dysfunctional family, and you have stepped toward the front and chosen a program for living. You are not them anymore unless you choose to be."

That hit me hard, and it literally hit home. I never lost sight of that. And I'm grateful she was brave enough to tell me what I needed to hear, that we are not defined by our past or circumstances. This was true liberation.

This sense of having the power to make choices and affect the behavior of those around me instilled within me a sense of dignity that had been missing—one that I still carry to this day.

Lane knew addiction, and she knew recovery. She was intimately familiar with the family-of-origin issues. One time during a family group, Lane confronted my mom, telling her emphatically that anything she did to enable me would be life-threatening. "He'll die, Joan," she proclaimed. "If you don't grasp the nature of how critical it is for Steven to break all these patterns and not be enabled, he will die. You will definitely end up burying your son!" The room was quiet while I cried.

She explained to me that if I ever relapsed, I would have to get completely sober again because abstinence was absolutely the only remedy for the disease. Years later, I would more clearly understand what she was saying: I must always fight for my life.

Rays of Light—Recovery in The Meadows:

We are not alone.

Prayers of every sort are answered, one way or another.

Prayer works.

God knows us, and He loves us.

The stakes are highest when the obstacle is greatest.

In the face of adversity, we will be carried if need be... always.

STUDY 4:
RECOVERY IN THE
MEADOWS

(Picture-perfect recovery)

Introduction:

When we really look at that individual, we just can't seem to get away from in the mirror, what do we see? We can never evade nor outrun the reality of who we are and what we have experienced. However, we can face ourselves and change the conversation so we can address the self-imposed lies and betrayals. In doing so, self-care, love, and speaking blessings to ourselves become the basis for our daily self-engagement. In other words, as the old proverb goes, "Fear comes calling, faith answers the door, and no one is there."

If you could visualize what recovery looks like, how would you describe it?

For the first three studies, we have looked at ourselves, evaluated what has contributed to our addiction, and have begun putting the foundational pieces in their right places to ensure we are headed toward recovery. For me, this was a huge turning point, and I needed to visualize what recovery looked like—otherwise I would only focus on what I feel or am facing at the moment. We all need to have something we focus on, a goal to shoot for, or something we push for when times get tough, because that is what we see ourselves working toward to be happy and healthy. This study will focus on the elements that make up recovery. The intriguing part of capturing this now is how much better it will be for you once you get to the other side and look back. It will be much more beautiful than you first described. Plus, if you record this now, it gives you another example to look back and see your progress... something to compare and encourage you to keep going. So let's get started!

Step 1: What's the setup?

We all have our own ideas of what the perfect setting will be when we reach recovery. Going through the process to recovery is hard work, but when we can picture what life will look like, that is often what keeps us going. In this first step, I would like you to do just that. Where are the top three places you will see the most dramatic change in your life? (Examples: Home, a new job, neighborhood, etc.)

List those here:

1._____

2._____

3._____

Step 2: How will you feel?

Sometimes focusing on the positive feelings we will have in recovery gives us enormous strength because we have often been faced with negative feelings brought on by our condition or experiences. What are the top three emotions you will feel once you have begun this journey of recovery and discovery? Explain why those are so important to you.

1._____

2._____

3._____

Step 3: Here's my big hope.

Each of us ultimately has a larger-than-life dream. These aren't lost or unknown to God. In fact, He knows what we most want and what His best is for us. Once we fully understand this and see it play out again and again, we can set our pace to walk fully into recover.

Here's your chance to visualize that dream. You see what's around you; you can feel what it's like to be in recovery... what is the one thing you dream for that just seems beyond comprehension for yourself?

My ultimate dream in recovery is:

_____

And why? (Describe this in as much detail as you can):

_____

Encouragement and Wisdom:

"If we confess our sins, he is faithful and just and will forgive us our sins and purify us from all unrighteousness." 1 John 1:9

"And God is able to bless you abundantly, so that in all things at all times, having all that you need, you will abound in every good work." 2 Corinthians 9:8

"His divine power has given us everything we need for a godly life through our knowledge of him who called us by his own glory and goodness." 2 Peter 1:3

Last Step: Let's reflect.

An "attitude of gratitude" has a nice ring to it and is served up early and often as you are submerged into the world of recovery. That phrase applies for every juncture of any element you are tackling where issues are concerned. Finding the best and the brightest parts even during dark moments helps to tune in the much-needed perspective button you must push when there's a challenge on the horizon. This helps us to clearly remember that often our worst days in recovery are better than our best days before we had Christ in our lives and sobriety.

In my early recovery time, it was essential for me to focus on what God had done for me and what He was currently doing in my life. That resulted in me painting the picture of a perfect meadow with me in it and feeling such perfect peace, something I never had in my life and was the farthest thing from what I knew.

As you reflect on your perfect picture of recovery, take this picture and describe it in your prayer time with God. Have a great conversation describing every aspect of this with Him as you pray. Take time to see it, smell it, and focus on what this will be like. This will give you another level of strength in your journey. Build on the promise that God will change your life if you focus on Him, do your part, and keep the conversation going with Him every day.

My note of encouragement to you:

As you continue to amass remarkable building blocks, take comfort in realizing there are many tools you are stockpiling in your toolbox. At times this will all just seem to be "too much." Take comfort… it is not. There will be moments when you feel (and rightfully so) that you have no answers and do not know what to do. That's a false message on play. Amidst those moments, you must stop, reflect, pray, give thanks, and know you have this. The best is yet to come. You are equipped and prepared.

CHAPTER 5
THE FALL

"Self-seeking will slip away."
Alcoholics Anonymous: Promises #8[ix]

My time in The Meadows and my re-entry into the world after those forty-two days were well-thought-out and very specific. First off, a common practice "post-treatment" is to enter some type of sober living facility. In my case, I pleaded for the ability to jump back into the care of my therapist and commit to a "90 in 90," which means attending ninety Alcoholics Anonymous meetings for ninety days in a row. The concern was that at my young age, there was a high probability of relapse, especially since my friends and contacts were not practicing sobriety. But after some deliberation, the cumulative decision was to take this route. Retrospectively I can see how the following twelve years were all perfectly aligned as part of Christ's continuing education for me on this early leg of my journey. I was not a Christ-follower at that point, but I believe that God orchestrated the circumstances of my life to prepare me for entrance into His kingdom and for the work I would one day do for Him.

This next part of the story is composed of many new life experiences, like moving to better places, wonderful sponsors investing in my life, remarkable periods of growth, and eventually a very serious engagement to a much older woman. My career trajectory sky-rocketed, and I morphed from a fledgling student into a sober, competent, gifted, successful, and driven young professional living life to its fullest. I was a rising star in the family-owned time-share company my father founded and developed. I always had a burning desire to perform, and this factor was to become my front-and-center spot where the light shined brightly upon me. I was volatile, unreasonable, unmanageable, and sober, and I brought tremendous results. Please note all the "I"s on that list. I was firmly entrenched in the idea that the entire world revolved around me, and I was equally certain I made it rotate. Since humility is a critical and sacred component of sobriety, the absence of it, especially over a sustained amount of time, is a precursor to utter disaster. I preferred to be heard and found that I had very little time or willingness to listen. I was utterly unreachable and beyond arrogant during this period.

I was living a textbook example of a common syndrome broadly recognized throughout A.A. as the ominous trilogy of "restless, irritable, and discontent". The common terminology for an individual in recovery displaying these traits is a "dry drunk." Usually, a sponsor, group member, or close friend in recovery will point this out (from a great distance) to the active offender. I had none of the above because I had become more and more disengaged from the world of recovery and more fully immersed in the world of Steven. It was rapidly turning into a darker place—a place so far from the core values and the gratitude that had initially delivered me to sobriety. In essence, I was a mess.

The void had retreated to the shadows but was still a poignant and ominous foreshadowing of the impending doom I was creating. Strangely enough, I continued to maintain a relationship with a higher power whom I chose to just call God. I did not acknowledge, nor did I know Christ the Lord. Jesus was not the focus of my spiritual life or even a name that entered my mind or left my mouth during this critical period. My Heavenly Father was and always has been there with me, but I had no idea what had been done for me or the enormous sacrifice that had been made on my behalf.

As time went on, I got further away from true reliance, even on God. There's another acronym in sobriety I love, EGO, which stands for "Edging God Out". At the time, I was perceived as having everything by anyone who saw my lifestyle, but I desperately lacked any type of real relationship with my Lord and Savior and the safety He provides. Instead, I broke off my engagement and continued on in an exciting new life as a bachelor, enjoying all the trappings of success and opportunities that came from living in Los Angeles. These changes became key elements in ensuring the impending doom I was rushing into would be massive.

I had freedom, money, and women. I also had droves of people working for me who would have jumped off a building with me and for me. But I could not buy enough or be enough to keep the darkness away. Slowly but surely, as my success continued to grow, my recovery continued to fade. The foundation that sobriety had built in me shifted away, yet I still felt powerful and empowered through self-will. The proverbial clock ticked loudly, but I failed to stop and recognize how hopelessly vulnerable I was. I forgot that every grateful recovering addict and alcoholic must hold on for dear life. My incurable disease waited patiently for the best moment to strike and unleash its fury after years, days, or even moments of neglect. One of the hardest things about being an addict is suffering from an illness that is very good at convincing me that I don't have an illness.

I seem to be referencing quite a few A.A. terms that fit well into this part of my story. One that again fits the bill describes a crucial safeguard against relapse and demise, "an attitude of gratitude". That was gone from my life during this period. I became unwilling to acknowledge any kind of thankfulness. Instead, I was angry and felt slighted, but I didn't know who I was angry with or why. I was constantly on edge and looking for a fight—anyone near me, whether or not I knew them, would fall victim to the poison I often spewed.

It came to the point where there was very little left in me of the peace and joy I had first found in sobriety. A.A. articulates the beautiful facets of sobriety I was quickly losing in a declaration of hope and truth called "The Promises." Generally, people who stay sober, even "dry drunks" like I was, will continue to experience some benefits of The Promises. They are:

The Promises

1. If we are painstaking about this phase of our development, we will be amazed before we are halfway through.

2. We are going to know a new freedom and a new happiness.

3. We will not regret the past nor wish to shut the door on it.

4. We will comprehend the word serenity and we will know peace.

5. No matter how far down the scale we have gone, we will see how our experience can benefit others.

6. That feeling of uselessness and self-pity will disappear.

7. We will lose interest in selfish things and gain interest in our fellow men and women.

8. Self-seeking will slip away.

9. Our whole attitude and outlook upon life will change.

10. Fear of people and economic insecurity will leave us.

11. We will intuitively know how to handle situations which used to baffle us.

12. We will suddenly realize that God is doing for us what we could not do for ourselves.

(From *The Big Book of Alcoholics Anonymous*, p. 83-84)[x]

Are these extravagant promises? Many of us who have been there don't think so. They are always being fulfilled among recovering addicts—sometimes quickly, sometimes slowly. Part of the beauty of the change demanded by recovery and the gifts it delivers is that these promises will always materialize if we accept the discipline and humility needed to get them. It sounds amazing, and in many ways, some of this was the amazing reality of my life during the twelve years that passed after my first trip to the bottom.

The day came when the promises for me vanished, and it started out like any other. Because of the way I had been living my life, I had no spiritual or mental defenses to warn me about the coming danger. Again, this was such a significant event in my life that I remember the start of my relapse after twelve years of uninterrupted sobriety as if it were a moment ago. A narcotic pill, a stronger version of Vicodin, was offered to me by a "friend". I didn't need it, nothing particularly hurt, and yet I took it. This moment is so clear that I can recall exactly how that orange, oblong-shaped pill looked in my hand. I hesitated for a tiny moment that had the power to alter my entire existence permanently... and then I swallowed it. In the world of sobriety and abstinence, that single event is called a relapse, a "slip". The door to full-blown addiction was open the moment I put the pill into my mouth, and I knew I was no longer sober.

I could have gone charging to an A.A. meeting even though I hadn't been to one in years—but I should have found one and been there that day taking a newcomer's chip.

A newcomer's chip is a circular chip or token given to anyone who attends an A.A. meeting for the first time or who is trying to start over to put their lives back together from a relapse. When given one of these chips, it helps everyone in the group know these are your first steps, and for those who are further into recovery to encourage and mentor you to continue.

I could have started again at that moment, but that was not to be my path. The beast, the disease lurking within exacted its revenge on my world by claiming everything it wanted. The eye of the storm careened toward me through cloaks of darkness, choking out more light than ever before. In a vacuum of light, *the void* opened its mouth wide and devoured me entirely. This time it would require nothing short of everything, and the intention of that emptiness was ultimately to see my life end. There was no salvation in sight. I had reentered treacherous and lethal waters that would seek to claim me without any reprieve. There was no turning back, there was no mercy, there was nothing but *the void*, and I felt completely lost to its power and control.

I speak now from the vantage point of time, looking backward. What is lost in a storm of this caliber will be everything, and therein lies *the beginning of the answer to all things.*

Rays of Light—The Fall:

Gratitude is imperative.

Remission from darkness, despair, and the destitution of evil is found through acts of humility and intentional obedience.

Misery is progressive and fully reversible.

STUDY 5:
THE FALL

(What are your stumbling blocks?)

Introduction:

Look at this moment as an entry ramp, a road to allow yourself access to a journey of acceptance. The slogans and sayings have merit here and offer great insight. "Those who forget the past are destined to repeat it." "If you go to the barber shop long enough, you're bound to get a haircut." "Never leave before the miracle…" Bumper stickers and billboards abound that spew appropriately worded sentiments that perfectly describe the map to this road we seek.

Talking Points:

I want to take a moment to let you know how proud I am of you.

I believe one of the strongest moments for me during my recovery was to realize I had to have a healthy fear of falling back into my addiction. Knowing that was as real to me then as it will be for every day for the rest of my life. It's a fact that if we ever let down our guards, we can find ourselves stumbling backwards. Because of that—we know we must be determined to not let that happen. Today I am stronger than when I was in my journey of recovery, and I use my determination to help others know they can do this. I call out the stumbling blocks so there is never a fall. I address them, and that way there isn't a casual effort or any wiggle room because I know what a fall will bring.

My encouragement to you as we go through this study is to look at this as identifying a problem you won't let lead to another fall. I am determined to help you make it and stay in the picture-perfect recovery you painted in the last session. Are you with me? Let's do it!

Step 1: What's the harm?

How many times have you bought into the lie of what you know will ultimately be your path to destruction? In one of the upcoming studies, we will discuss how your actions will ultimately be the breaking of a long, painful legacy in your family. You will become the strongest leader your family or circle of influence has ever known, all because you were determined to lead with good choices and not allow yourself to fall. That said, what are the most likely places you can see as crossroads you might face that could potentially lead you stumbling into another fall?

List those here:

1._____

2._____

3._____

Step 2: Not on my watch!

You can call it before it would happen, and you most likely already know how to avoid the situations you listed above. But for assurance for yourself, as a leader, name what you would do differently to avoid these stumbling blocks above. If you could write the playbook, what would you tell yourself you must do to avoid these?

List as many things you can do to help give you a plan of attack.

1._____

2._____

3._____

Step 3: The enemy in the camp.

Sometimes we face things we don't expect, especially when not everyone around us wants to see us succeed. There is evil in this world. It is best to say it and accept it. But the good news is that you're never alone, and most importantly, you have God on your side if you trust in His protection over your life. He will not allow an enemy to overpower you.

The Bible talks about an enemy that roams the earth and works through people who don't know or love God to bring hardship and destruction to our lives. God's promise is that if we believe and trust in Him, He will not allow our enemies to overcome us.

Today we want to take an important step. If you haven't already, we want to encourage you to invite God to be the Lord of your life, to come into your heart, and to protect your every step. Today, take a step toward reaching total recovery by asking Him to protect you, save you from your past, and lead you forward because you completely put your trust in Him.

If you already have done this—then I am encouraging you to spend time asking God to protect you from your enemies, to keep you safe while you're recovering, and to lead you forward with each day.

In both cases, I want to congratulate you. You just took advantage of the most powerful piece of this study. The journey is still before us, but you will find strength in each day as you grow forward.

I am proud of you!

Take a moment and send me an email or message via our website to let us know that you have taken that step and proclaimed Christ as your savior. My team and I promise to add you to our growing prayer list where we celebrate each decision like you made today.

Wahoo!

Encouragement and Wisdom:

"Very truly I tell you, whoever hears my word and believes him who sent me has eternal life and will not be judged but has crossed over from death to life." John 5:24

"This, then, is how you should pray: 'Our Father in heaven, hallowed be your name, your kingdom come, your will be done, on earth as it is in heaven. Give us this day our daily bread, and forgive us our debts, as we also have forgiven our debtors. And lead us not into temptation, but deliver us from the evil one.'" Matthew 6: 9-13

"But the Lord is faithful, and he will strengthen you and protect you from the evil one. We have confidence in the Lord that you are doing and will continue to do the things we command. May the Lord direct your hearts into God's love and Christ's perseverance." 2 Thessalonians 3:3-5

Last Step: Let's reflect.

There is an answer, solution, and a resolution—a simple formula for complicated individuals. The remedy for what ails us is through our Creator. We will be granted a remission from our suffering based on our spiritual condition. In the depths of my greatest despair, as I emerged from the abyss to gasp a breath, I called out to Jesus Christ. I asked Him to take my life into his hands and committed that I would spend my days from that point forward serving Him best, first. The darkness transcended into light. I could see and in my heart I knew—if I lived that prayer, if I turned to the Lord, if I gathered my greatest strength by owning my greatest weakness—I would be given a life beyond any simple expectations I carried.

In recovery, facing head on what we already know are our weaknesses and stumbling blocks prepares us for when they come. Putting our trust in God and asking Him into our lives completely fills *the void* that we all have when we are born.

It's God's plan to provide us with the assurance that we don't have to live with stumbling blocks, disappointment, pain, and the other things that try to steal what He had planned for us. It starts with us making the right choices and growing in the way He intended for us.

Today, take time to pray for all the things you are thankful for, how God will work in your life, how He already has, and how He will help you grow going forward.

My note of encouragement to you:

Your worth is unparalleled. You are loved beyond comprehension. The lies that have followed you (us) are just that, LIES! There is a Holy Spirit and a community of so many waiting for you, praying, and walking with you. Some are right there in front of you, and some are yet unknown. We all find one another, and the gift of that community bridges the proverbial gap we have been scrambling to cover. Go forward boldly. If you don't feel you're ready, let me provide a moment of courage for you. He endured the cross for you and me. He overcame the world for us—this world where He told us we would have trouble. He has the kingdom waiting for us, but it lives within our hearts. As we journey further, more shall be revealed. I have said it before and I will state it again: "I have a God who loves you, and I love you, too!"

CHAPTER 6
RELAPSE, DESPAIR, AND THE BOTTOM

"No matter how far down the scale we have gone,
we will see how our experience can benefit others."
Alcoholics Anonymous: Promise #5[xi]

From that first pill on, my use and ingestion increased daily. I subsequently relapsed into a paradigm of outlandish and repulsive behavior which methodically began to burn every bridge that twelve years of sobriety had constructed. I lost more touch with the realm of reality, while hurdling closer to a hard hit at the bottom, a destination of such hopelessness I could not have imagined. In sobriety, I had been granted a reprieve based on my healthy and formerly humble condition. Though I didn't know the Lord Jesus Christ at this point in my life, I did believe in a higher power that I called God. I was doing good work in A.A. I was sober. I even sponsored people, had a home group, and the promises were coming true in my life. That's the part of what long-term sobriety is based on, but because I didn't know God, pride stealthily crept back in. Because I wasn't anchored by a spiritual foundation or footing, I left myself vulnerable to stumble, Ultimately, I fell hard to the bottom.

These are the trappings that everyone in recovery faces and starts to believe in their own success instead of trusting in God's leading to heal them from their disease.

Sobriety provides you with the basic elements that tell you everything is okay. But your disease is like a second version of yourself who is working against you, determined to see you get off track and relapse.

It's a vicious cycle that addicts war within themselves. We aren't equipped to go at this alone.

In my weakness, the constant lies of alcoholism and drug addiction had no trouble chaining me right back into absolute slavery. Like the beautiful voices of Ulysses's sirens trying to tempt him to come off course, these lies lulled me with constant affirmations that I did not have a disease. As a result, I lost sight of myself. I focused on the shell of my accomplishments, and my disease came back ten times worse than before, strong enough to drive me to my bottom and, ultimately, to the most pivotal point in my life.

One of the biggest changes in the "second time around" was in what and how I used. Cocaine was the focal point of my relapse. The mental effects of this poison, combined with a high volume of pill use, led to literally insane behavior and the quick exit of everyone and everything in my life. At the end of this second fall, as I described in the first chapter, I suffered from extremely vivid, paranoid, delusional episodes, in addition to feeling unbearably isolated. The voices I heard as I ingested cocaine contributed to my feeling I had lost my sanity. I would hear almost a narrative of someone observing what I was doing. These "voices" or "people" proclaimed things like, "Well, we're at it again. He's using. He sits in his apartment all day and night and uses."

These incidents both enraged me and terrified me. Many times, I would hear the voices state that they would call the authorities on me. This led to terror and anxiety so extreme that I would literally be paralyzed with fear. I was afraid that if I moved, "they" would hear me, and "they" would know I heard them. Even as I write this, my body remembers the physical sensation that passed through me during these episodes. The feelings of despair were so tangible and utterly terrifying. In such a state of panic, simple acts like leaving home or showering were far too terrifying to endure. Delusion and delirium grew to such a massive extent that during the brief moments (and they were literally moments) when I wasn't using, I would go somewhere else hoping to get away from these people and their intolerable narrative.

One of the most impactful events at that time was the loss of my livelihood. Although my siblings and I now held principal ownership in our lucrative family company, my father sent my termination paperwork to me via FedEx. Based on my conduct, he made what I view now as a life-saving call, because enabling an addict is basically writing their death sentence. I would never start climbing up and out until I could go no further down. Though this may seem counter-intuitive, letting me go from my job was the best way to help me.

After my termination, all the trappings and blessings of what I had worked for disappeared one by one. Stereotypical elements present in the life of an active addict and alcoholic are profoundly accurate, and I had them all: the flashy car, the fancy apartment, the clothing, and the jewelry. I lost or sold all of it quickly to feed the monster within. These things had never satisfied my emptiness when I had them, and now what little they provided in the way of cash didn't come close to quenching the insatiable appetite of my raging addiction.

My behavior became not just physically violent, but verbally as well. I lashed out at everyone around me and began vicious campaigns of phone calls and emails—many of those directed at my father and other family members. I even began the process of a lawsuit and action against the family business. These repulsive actions, along with ongoing threats and proclamations to all of them that I would kill myself, broke every important relationship in my life to the point where no one would talk to me. The impact and fallout of my actions—once they had settled— left me sitting in the dust and rubble with nothing to show for it, a picture of true emptiness. I was paralyzed, unable to function in the sight of society, heartbroken, financially wiped out, spiritually bankrupt, and alone.

All of these factors led me to that fateful night of November 11, 2004, when I ingested a combination of drugs and alcohol that no human body could survive without supernatural intervention. Looking back, there isn't one part of my walk that I would choose to alter because this was the groundwork needed to bring me to my knees. This was the mangled road that humbled me and inspired my desperate and heartfelt plea to my Lord and Savior Jesus Christ for deliverance.

Inexplicably, I lived through that night, and when I called out to God to save me, Jesus, the light of heaven, gave me a new life... my true life as a child of the living God. All along there had been a plan, a purpose, and a charted course that would ultimately bring glory to God's kingdom. Through His grace and mercy, I was set onto the path that He, my Heavenly Father, had been preparing and waiting to set me on all along. He spared my life and delivered me into this new life miraculously whole, in my right mind, and with the strength to proclaim His glory... and by my estimation, all for the sake of those who are still lost in *the void*.

Rays of Light—Relapse, Despair, the Bottom:

It's never as dark as before the dawn.

Those who forget the past are destined to repeat it.

All of it is always for His glory and the glory of His kingdom.

Being driven to your knees is a good place to be.

Cry out to Jesus for help. You will be heard, you will be helped, and you will be made whole again.

STUDY 6:
RELAPSE, DESPAIR, AND THE BOTTOM

Introduction:

There is a blueprint for your life... a plan, if you will. Many of these plans have remarkable similarities, though the beauty often is in the remarkable differences. Everyone has their own. Make no mistake, there is a formula and a way to succeed, not succumb to the load.

Again, Faith without works is dead (James 2). To move forward in faith, we must execute a moment at a time and a day at a time to ensure the result. There is an answer to breaking through the chaos of your addiction. Let's look at the actions to fill in that infinite blank of "how to"

In the last session we talked about stumbling blocks and having the right motivation with determination instilled so we don't stumble. Let's add a little more weight into how important this area is to keep on our radar each day.

Step 1: Daily motivation.

Consider making these keywords and phrases a part of your motivation for each day:

1. Be intentional.

2. Determination.

3. My resolve is set and will not change.

4. I am consistent and won't waiver.

Step 2: Five key points.

This week's study is more of my one-on-one coaching directly to you to ensure you don't fail. I am praying for you and will continue to do so. I am confident that if you understand how dire the circumstances can be if you have a relapse, it will create in you a healthy fear to never allow it to happen. For me, it was a matter of life or death. Yours could be the same, but it's my prayer never to see this happen as long as you believe in the Lord, trust in the process, and make the right choices.

Point 1: Whatever you have been granted in reprieve, if you don't stay on course it will come back ten times worse in a relapse. Can you imagine being ten times worse than you are?

God warns us about this in the Bible when He talks about unclean evil in our lives. If we aren't careful, we make it that much worse for ourselves when we relapse.

"Then it says, 'I will return to the house I left.' When it arrives, it finds the house unoccupied, swept clean and put in order. Then it goes and takes

with it seven other spirits more wicked than itself, and they go in and live there. And the final condition of that person is worse than the first. That is how it will be with this wicked generation." Matthew 12:44-45

Point 2: You must acknowledge, make a pledge to yourself, or create a contract to put weight to the words here. What does that look like?

I, _____, am committed to not allow myself to return to what was killing me and robbing me of the life that I now have in Christ. I pledge to be consistent each day with prayer, reading God's word, and never allowing myself to take any steps, no matter how small, where they would be leaning toward a relapse. I trust the Lord with my life and my protection. I seal this with God's promise over my life.

Signed _____

Point 3: Your resolve is everything. You've now made a pledge with yourself, but it means nothing unless you live up to it. That means your heart must be committed to ensuring you will do whatever it takes each day not to relapse. I have a daily routine vital to my living a peaceful, recovered life. If it helps you, then write this out and review it every day until you have it memorized.

Point 4: Routines are critical. None of us like to live in ruts, but routines ensure we stay consistent with the things crucial to our survival.

If you knew you had to have a daily transfusion to survive, you would be sure not to miss your appointment. This is how important a daily routine is to your survival. My word to you is to stick with it and use your success as your way to help show others who struggle with any of these things you struggle with—there is a path to recovery.

Point 5: This is what I have done and how it worked for me. Let me share from my experience.

Prayer is my starting and ending point of each day. In the morning when I rise, I ask the Lord to please keep me sober. I then pray for others in need and for things I want to do that will ultimately serve Him and His kingdom best. I surrender my will and striving in my day by turning things over to Him. In doing so, I put the day and the outcome into His hands and trust in the results. At night I pray again to thank Him for my day and revisit my prayers to see what He did this day and to offer my gratitude. I pray in the evening to ask for forgiveness in any area where I have fallen short.

In addition, during my day, I do my best to reach out intentionally to others. I do this without expectation of anything in return. One of the significant facts in recovery is how self-healing it can be to give to others, as it offers us a reprieve from ourselves. I practice self-care throughout my day with what I eat, physical activity, patience, and love.

This balanced recipe for me and when done right or even at a "medium" level, it provides great peace and serenity. I encourage you to find your own plan that works for you so you can safeguard your step and maximize each moment with your peace of mind.

Encouragement and Wisdom:

"Submit yourselves, then, to God. Resist the devil, and he will flee from you." James 4:7

"I have the right to do anything, you say - but not everything is beneficial. I have the right to do anything - but I will not be mastered by anything." 1 Corinthians 6:12

"And the God of all grace, who called you to his eternal glory in Christ, after you have suffered a little while, will himself restore you and make you strong, firm and steadfast." 1 Peter 5:10

Last Step: Let's reflect.

We are loved, and our Heavenly Father is present. I want to urge you and encourage you to grasp the reality that you are not alone. The Lord is always present. He is willing to care for you and wants a relationship with you. He knows us all, and He always has. Like an earthly father, our Heavenly Father yearns to hear from His children. I understand far too well that feeling that He couldn't possibly be focused on me or care. I thought so many times, "If He had been there, then the journey I had would have never happened." I know now He has a plan for me and that all things work together for His purpose here on earth and in heaven. You will see and feel His presence the more you turn toward Him and put it all in His hands. It is by trusting and knowing that you are His child and He is orchestrating all of this for your best, for our best, and for the glory of His kingdom that will demonstrate your faith.

My note of encouragement to you:

This part of the study guide will be one of the most important parts of the work we are doing. It will grow and continue to develop within you and through you. I want you to know a part of my daily and nightly prayers now are praying for you. Yes, I'm praying for your steps of recovery.

Anyone who takes these words to heart and applies them will receive everything they need to help aid them in whatever they are facing.

I am praying for your comfort and peace amidst any storm you may be facing, as well as the strength to continue on by faith. Maybe you feel you have never had anyone pray for you. Rest assured you are covered in prayer, and we know the power of prayer works. Each day and night I'm in prayer for you and yours in Christ's name for the glory of His kingdom.

CHAPTER 7
MY OWN BRAND
OF DIGNITY

"We will intuitively know how to handle situations
which used to baffle us."
Alcoholics Anonymous: Promises #11[xii]

If you have ever been detained underwater a little longer than you wanted to be, then you know the joy of filling your lungs with oxygen the moment you break through. With the same joy and relief, and from November 12, 2004 onward, the world became a beautiful place for me to live. I had a roof over my head and very little else, but now with Christ living in my heart, it just didn't matter.

My rebirth and being given new life through grace brought me renewed hope, peace, clarity, and wisdom. I now understood that it was one building block after another, and they all fit together as God intended the course of my life. Grace had moved in, and I embraced it.

First, I became engrossed in prayer. I would tell my Heavenly Father openly that, while I didn't understand His grace and mercy, I accepted it and would trust Him by going where that grace and mercy took me. Little, simple things became opportunities for unparalleled gratitude. For instance, the absence of the horrible voices was reason alone for moment-to-moment joy in my day. The ability to shower and go outside was also remarkable. I embraced these daily acts with the excitement of a child who had reached a significant benchmark. I was filled with wonder, liberated by my creator and grateful beyond words.

The resuscitation of my physical health followed that of my spiritual well-being. I had been so destitute of resources that a monthly gym membership was beyond my reach. However, my beloved mother, Joan, knew I was sober and mercifully signed me up at one I could walk to from my apartment. I dove back into the familiarity of weights and cardio…lots and lots of cardio. Music always was and still is a huge part of my workout. Back in those days, I didn't realize that God's Holy Spirit was wrapping me up tight while I worked out. Tears upon tears would flow at the gym. I didn't care who saw, or how it appeared; I was just so filled with glee, gratitude, and hope as those streams of pain and relief fell down my face while I worked out.

Employment was the next to come back into my life. I joyfully started doing all sorts of jobs as soon as I found an opportunity. For instance, I taught spin at the gym I belonged to, with zero certification. My classes were known to be filled with inspirational speeches, music, and enthusiasm, and people were always lined up to get in. I loved talking with the people in my classes and weaving in messages of hope and inspiration as we all spun and perspired. There were numerous examples like this during the first year of my second sobriety. These vocational blessings never provided substantial income, but they filled my heart and soul with a joy that no amount of financial gain could compare.

Then the transformation took shape as I became focused on others. I wanted to share the love and blessings in my heart with people I met on a daily basis because I was no longer terrified, paralyzed with fear, panicked, or intoxicated. I felt light in my heart, and there was a constant bounce in my step. I didn't know enough then to realize that the Holy Spirit was literally encompassing me with love and nurturing me back to being whole. But at the same time, I was acutely aware of the Lord's fingerprints all over the things that occurred during this period.

"God Shots" is a term from A.A. used to describe miraculous provisions from God given to us along the journey of our lives. I experienced a significant one roughly six months into my sobriety when I started thinking it would be wise to get a medical examination to see what shape my body was left in after years of destruction. There had been such extreme ingestion of cocaine and pills that despite feeling strong and well, I was certain the abuse on my body had resulted in something serious like permanent organ damage. I started saving money so I could make a walk-in appointment at an independent urgent care facility in my Westwood neighborhood. At the same time, I started preparing myself mentally for the worst. I had priced the visit and the labs, mustered some funds. After the initial consultation, exam, and lab work, I had a return visit the following week to hear the results.

At that return visit, the doctor greeted me with a perplexed expression on his face. Since I was scared already, I immediately assumed they had found something awful and that he was trying to find the best way to tell me. I am happy to say I turned out to be very wrong!

First, he asked if I were seeking a claim or trying to build a case of some sort. I explained I simply wanted to assess my condition after years of substance abuse. He went on to tell me that based on that explanation, and with what I had already told him about my history, the results of my test did not medically add up. My counts were "remarkable." Both my physical and lab-based exam showed I was a picture of pristine health. He was shocked, pleased, and unsure why I would be motivated to lie about my past—if indeed I were. After hearing all this, I told him that I had been saved by Jesus Christ and that this was the reason my results didn't match my former, extreme level of self-abuse.

This heartfelt declaration seemed to confound the doctor to an even greater degree than my physical wellbeing. He looked up from my chart and said, "Ginsburg...that's Jewish?"

"Yes," I told him.

He replied, "Jesus Christ? How did that happen?"

"I've been blessed with a miracle, Sir," I explained to this kind (and yes, Jewish) doctor. "This visit to you and these results are all part of it."

Today I realize clearly that the miracle of recovery was exactly what had been occurring during my first months of sobriety. Years of self-abuse were being shed away as blessings of physical, spiritual, and mental progress were added at an accelerated pace every day.

Along with the victory of each small accomplishment I made toward sobriety and regaining my physical health, by God's amazing grace, the massive divide that my illness had created between my family and me gradually diminished. In fact, as I headed toward my ninth month of sobriety, the relationship that had incurred the most damage was miraculously restored.

My father and I had been pushed worlds apart through the addiction-fueled actions of my hands and words of my mouth. My stepmother Rosemarie, a believer, knew that her faithful prayers for almost the entire time she had known me had been answered when I entered sobriety again and committed my life to Jesus Christ. As things progressed, she broached the subject of reconciliation with my father. This was not inherently something my dad was interested in, and I couldn't blame him one bit. I had wreaked monumental havoc on my entire family, especially where my Dad was concerned. All of this being said, my stepmother, who loves me as her own and loves Jesus, proclaimed the following to my dad, "Your son is sober, your son needs and wants you, and your son has found Jesus Christ."

I believe from A to Z, this was all beyond disconcerting to my father. As he declared to my stepmother that there would be no reconciliation, she explained to him that he would need to pack. My father was confused because at that moment, though he traveled often for work, he did not have a trip planned. She explained that if he would not reach out for us to come back together, then he would have to move out because it was unacceptable for him to not offer me grace. The next day, my Father and I were on the phone. We have never looked back, and we have rebuilt a relationship that supersedes anything I had ever known with my dad before.

Christ was and is at the center of this critical loop being closed. The massive progress I have made has been a daily journey with the power that comes from walking with Jesus. As the days, weeks, and months passed, the foundation of the Lord's love and light grew stronger within me as my confidence grew knowing I was His beloved child. Daily His power and wisdom worked in me to make amends for the devastation I caused others, and to abrogate the attempted, permanent harm I had sought to cause myself.

Christ inscribed on my heart that the purpose I was spared for is to love others in His name and to profess the greatness of His love and mercy for all mankind. Christ Jesus was the one who filled that infinite *void* each day in large and small ways, repeatedly proving that the lies I had believed and lived by were devoid of any substance or worth. I relished my path and stood, grateful for the journey my history placed me on. I boldly forged ahead each new day with a permanent gift of gratitude. I carried daily the great blessing of humility, to never forget who I was, where I had been and now through Him, where I will always be.

Rays of Light—My Own Brand of Dignity:

The Holy Spirit lives within us when we receive God's forgiveness.

The Lord's love is sustaining, fulfilling, and undeniable.

We are called to love one another.

By His power, our greatest travesties will lead us to triumph beyond measure.

Look at your life right now. The Lord's fingerprints are all over it, too.

STUDY 7:
MY OWN BRAND
OF DIGNITY

(My testimony is my redemption.)

Introduction:

To simply say there is so much to be gained fails to convey the glory and gift of what lay ahead for all of us as we trudge the road to happy destiny.

There are so many areas where we learn and grow as we start to love and live. Be bold and courageous. These are easy attributes to reference, yet challenging ones to execute consistently. Give yourself the gift of willingness. Take heart in the fact that it's truly a process and the work (yes, reclamation of the best of ourselves is **WORK**) will bear fruit and lead us to heights and realizations that exceed any of our expectations

This is a new day for you. This is your new day. This is your birthday, a fresh beginning.

One of my biggest areas to wrestle to the ground was a struggle with self-esteem. It started early in my life from what I witnessed in my family. I didn't believe in myself, nor did I understand that I was uniquely created by God, that He had a plan for my life, and I just needed to get to know Him and make Him Lord of my life.

This played itself out in so many areas of my life, and I started looking for ways to fill up that *void* where I just didn't feel like I measured up for anyone. I wish I had known then what I know now... that God—not drugs, circumstances, events, job, money or anything else—would fill what I was missing.

Today I understand that so much more and why it led to my event. Fifteen plus years later, I see the exact opposite unfolding in my life. I have much to be thankful for, and I am excited to see what God has for you. Filling *the void* in your life and getting rid of the pain you are trying to erase will only happen if you turn to God and allow Him to heal you through His plan.

Today I want you to think back over the past six sessions and expound a little more on what you feel contributed to your addiction. Was it self-esteem? What was it in your life that had you reach for something to ease your pain, to help you escape?

Take a few minutes and dig deep here. What do you think were the underlying contributing things that led to your addiction? If you're like me, your mind wanders. I often think of times when I fell short, felt shamed, or was made to feel less than who I was created to be. If I focus only on those times specifically, then everything else starts to disappear. I can easily remember the harsh words from others or see myself falling short. There were memories that brought me back to relive pivotal moments where I took the wrong fork in the road and ended up on the wrong path based on bad decisions.

These recollections hurt. They are steeped in remorse and filled with massive amounts of the "what could have been" and "if I only had." Let's be clear. These feelings, thoughts, or memories are filled with facts that we can tell ourselves, but they represent lies. The fact is that what happened actually happened and what we recall occurred. The lie is that those times will define who we will be and what we will do. That bondage of self is yesterday's news and has no place or power over any of us moving forward. Each day and moment we have comes with the ability through the Lord's grace and love to chart a new course. We can begin again to write a new page in a new chapter. All of this is part of what we produce based on who we are and who we will become through Christ.

Encouragement and Wisdom:

Read Acts 9:1-19. This is a story about someone named Saul who did horrible things (murder), and yet God redeemed him. He eventually became a leader through Christ who transformed his life. This type of transformation is what is going on with you and where you are headed.

"For he chose us in him before the creation of the world to be holy and blameless in his sight." Ephesians 1: 4

"Do not conform to the pattern of this world, but be transformed by the renewing of your mind. Then you will be able to test and approve what God's will is—his good, pleasing and perfect will." Romans 12:2

Last Step: Let's reflect.

What a gift to see ourselves and then love ourselves authentically for all that we are, for all that we were, and for all that we will be. I am in no position to ask you for anything. You have given so much just taking the time to do these exercises and read these words. My hope is that you be patient with yourself. None of us got to our breaking points where we needed help overnight. In addition, none of us can, nor will be able to correct what ails us overnight. Treat yourself well, be patient, be intentional, and take heart because the best is yet to come.

My note of encouragement to you:

Step by step, action by action, and often moment by moment we are moving forward in the Lord's name. We have hope, and that proverbial light we see at the end of the tunnel is not a train. Trust where you are being led and take an inventory of your progress on a regular basis. You are worth this work, and this work is worthy of you. You are not alone, nor are you a misfit. The exciting part is the discovery of what is yet to come. The hard work is what must be done to perpetuate that discovery, but it's worth it. Remember to tackle each day with action and a prayer at a time.

CHAPTER 8
THE OLD TAPES

"Our whole attitude and outlook upon life will change."
Alcoholics Anonymous: Promise #9[xiii]

"Those who forget the past are destined to repeat it." Even though it's not mine, I love this saying and think of it often when the past comes calling, uninvited and without warning. There will be moments (Praise the Lord they are just moments!) when a destructive collection of mental billboards with cruel labels with the most negative connotations possible about my history flood my heart and mind. Their material for making accusations against me come from the shame and pain that the Lord has pulled me through. The huge difference is that He only uses these same memories to help me learn and grow, rather than to condemn. These dark thoughts of hopelessness from the past play on repeat in my mind, squelching my joy and enveloping me so completely that I literally feel like I am not present. These messages from the past that twist my thoughts are pure lies.

I've found that certain factors make me more vulnerable to becoming a victim of these wicked condemnations. They come when I am weak in any way, so any overwhelming degree of hunger or fatigue is a catalyst. Any level of resentment I'm engrossed in can also be a producer of an old tape rearing its ugly head. Fortunately, I've found that one of the best and most immediate remedies to silence these hateful lies is prayer. When my past is impeding on my present, I beg God to be relieved of my burden of self. Sometimes, if one of these episodes is powerful enough, I might even say out loud to the condemning thought, "That's a lie!"

These lies have been penned by different authors: teachers, peers, camp counselors, other offenders, perpetrators, family members, all people who had opportunities to pen journal entries into the book of my life. They are a part of my history, but these words spoken or written to me are not the issue or the problem that caused me to choose addiction. Instead, I attribute any degree of pain that came from bad choices of the past directly to my lack of gratitude and rejection of God's grace at the time. In other words, the pain inflicted by my fall and relapses was self-imposed. Somewhere in all the mess of my life, I made choices.

It's great to know that the remedy for the pain I brought upon myself, because it was self-imposed, was countered with an answer that, not only was a remedy for the pain, but it started me on a path that could have only come through Christ Jesus... a path of true and lasting healing.

Now, as I have continued to surrender my life humbly to the Lord from the first moment I was aware of His presence, He brings maturity to my life by graciously opening my eyes to see that I have also played a part in the incidents that led to the pain. It's difficult to admit because I would rather not take any blame. Yet, I've come to accept that my true culpability will be a burden I carry for the rest of my life. I have been given too much in the way of life lessons for this to ever completely subside, so I live with it like a spiritual and emotional limp from an old injury. I'm very comfortable with this because the part that really matters to me is that the repercussions of these times do not affect or carry over to the ones I love. Christ's gift to me is that I'm here to break the chain of dysfunction in my family line. To that end, I offer my life and recovery as a testimonial to prove there is hope and a better way waiting and proven for anyone who would care to partake. I remain grateful to the Lord for everything He has given me and for the privilege to point the way.

This may sound strange to someone who has never walked a similar path as mine, but Nicole, my wife, and the children and I are best served through the episodes I've survived in my life. Through everything, God has shaped and molded my character, my heart, and my faith to be the person I am today. When the past becomes a paralyzing echo chamber with sounds of the failure reverberating from the past into my present, I consider them a cautionary omen. I have been waging war over a long period of time using the truth to combat lies as the primary weapon, and as a result, self-condemnation about my past has become more and more manageable. At the same time, I realize that my Heavenly Father needs the following pearl of wisdom to remain firmly entrenched in my mind:

"An ounce of prevention is worth a pound of cure."

I must and will continue to be mindful of the enemy's tactics against me as I am today, and I will remain, steeped in prayers of gratitude for where I have been, where I'm going, and where I will be. I do this for the sake of my Lord and Savior whom I serve, for the sake of those whom I love, and for the sake of my best days still to come for serving others.

Rays of Light—The Old Tapes:

When the past comes calling, prayer is the answer.

Self-talk and self-love are a gift from Christ.

What happened in the past is not what is happening in the present.

Spiritual disconnection will lead to being restless, irritable, and discontent.

I will fail those I love and serve if I let yesterday's mistakes ruin today's gifts.

STUDY 8:
THE OLD TAPES

(Despair will creep up—know it and be ready for it.)

Introduction:

There is a lyric I love in "Revelation Song" recorded in 2009 by Kari Jobe:

"Sing a new song to Him who sits on heaven's mercy seat."

Those words are so spot on, especially for someone in recovery. We must be intentional to change our personal songs. The Lord is waiting and wants to rectify our lives. It has been the missing piece or peace in our lives. Once we embrace this, it will continue to rectify our truths and empower us each day forward. Trust this truth. Live and see for yourself that this beautiful truth is the foundation of all that waits for us in this wonderful journey we are embarked upon.

Have you ever wondered why we have that voice in our head that discourages us? That kicks us down? That makes us think less of who we are and is the opposite of how God made us to be?

I know that these "Old Tapes" stem from our enemy, because they do not come from God. It can eat away at us and ultimately if we listen to it, then it can cause us to relapse or, worse yet, destroy us. Knowing we have an enemy that would want nothing more than this to happen, we have the power through Christ to not let these tapes play.

Instead, there is a new song, a song of praise and worship we can sing. We remind ourselves of the good things that happen through recovery, a new relationship with Christ in our hearts, and having God lead us every day. This session I want to focus on what the voices say to us and how we can overcome that.

What are three things that negative voice in your head (the old tapes) says to you?

1._____

2._____

3._____

How would you respond to this voice to stand firm in your position and your commitment to recovery?

1._____

2._____

3._____

What other things have you learned through this study that you can rely on to help give you strength?

1._____

2._____

3._____

Encouragement and Wisdom:

"Be alert and of sober mind. Your enemy the devil prowls around like a roaring lion, looking for someone to devour." 1 Peter 5:8

"Worship the Lord your God, and his blessing will be on your food and water. I will take away sickness from among you." Exodus 23:25

"Heal me, Lord, and I will be healed; save me and I will be saved, for you are the one I praise." Jeremiah 17:14

Last Step: Let's reflect.

Prayer can be such a complex and perplexing task for so many of us. I find prayer amongst other things to be a simple act for complicated people. The Lord doesn't have a right way that He wants to hear a prayer from us. He does, however, yearn for a relationship with us. How we pray, when we pray, and what we pray for is not about the words that are said.

What matters most is the relationship that comes through our talking with Him. Above all else, where all of these factors are concerned, PRAY.

I choose to pray from when I wake up until I call it a night. Our prayers are always heard and can be done anywhere and at any time; for example, when we are walking, when we are driving the car (they're especially important when we drive), and when we have a moment at work. Any time and all the time, we should pray. I believe in turning things over to God. I put whatever I'm dealing with in his hands and I ask Him to do his will. I pray with hope and a full heart, but I do my best to pray without expectations. As I continue to trudge ahead and as issues or circumstances are resolved, I always see God's part in the result, and I'm always grateful that I've prayerfully given it to Him. That's where our faith grows, and we learn by watching God work in our lives to trust Him. "Thy will be done" is a prayer. "I need you, Lord" is a great prayer. "Help me, I'm hurting, Father" (He is our loving, nurturing, and patient Heavenly Father.) is a hall of fame prayer.

Pray when you get angry, when you are happy, and when you are sad. Pray to put the Lord first in your life. Let Him lead and follow where He takes you. Remember, because you have prayer, you can never be alone or uncertain. The Lord loves to hear from us and is waiting with excitement because He loves us. In fact, He loves us beyond any words, and He wants

His best for us. To sum it up simply, He is Lord, He is ours, and we are His. Amen.

My note of encouragement to you:

Isn't it liberating to know that this new normal we choose to create is the sheer accessibility of it? As we have discussed, the Lord wants to hear from us. He doesn't care where or how we pray; He encourages us to just pray. Remember to free yourself up that there is no wrong way to pray. Certainly there are things that should not be the sole focus of our prayers, but it starts with our hearts and having time to talk with God. There are no limitations or any maximum capacity on our prayers.

Eventually, a church connection, music, small groups, and reading the Bible will all become tremendous seeds of growth in your prayer life. I'm excited to share the different facets of what's in my heart regarding prayer with you. I know that so much of the conviction I carry in my heart directly results from the Lord's answer to my hopes, my dreams, the Holy Spirit, and the calling out to my Heavenly Father in prayer.

I hope these words, which are absolutely a gift from Christ to me to you, liberate you. I pray you feel free to be vulnerable, to reach out to seek harbor in the hands of our creator. If you're looking for something to focus on during prayer, there's no downside to trying a prayer cycle. Take some days, nights, or whenever, and pray on something in your life. Watch what happens. Look at how it makes you feel and be mindful of how you are from that point forward in your day-to-day activities. I believe firmly and faithfully that you will see why there is so much praying going on. I love prayer, and I love talking about prayer. I'm excited about your prayer life wherever it leads you. I am praying for you, and we have a God that loves you and loves us. What a gift !

CHAPTER 9
MY PRECIOUS GIFTS

"We will lose interest in selfish things
and gain interest in our fellows."
Alcoholics Anonymous: Promise #7[xv]

There have been countless gifts and blessings from the concurrent moment my sobriety and my relationship with the Lord began. My health, work, placement back into my family, and my ability to pour into the community were the best part of many treasures I was given. Yet none of these carry any comparison to the blessing the Lord bestowed upon me when He brought my spectacular wife, Nicole, into my life.

The day I met Nicole, there were people in my life who had known me for a long time. They knew all about me. I turned to them and proclaimed, "I'm going to marry that girl...that's my wife!" There may have been some repressed laughter, but they did all compliment me on my outlook and commended me for "thinking the right way." Those same lovely people explained that the whole "Jesus thing" was terrific and that the world was certainly a better and safer place with me being clean and sober again; but in their minds, reality had to be grasped, especially where someone like Nicole was concerned. They went on to explain that Nicole, being the person they knew her to be, would not be marrying me. But my head was in the right place, and Christ was at work. Six months later, Nicole and I were engaged.

The miracle of that alone is obvious to those blessed enough to encounter my remarkable, godly wife. Those same people often wonder how that feat occurred. Nicole is so centered, balanced, and present, yet she went ahead and managed to fall in love with and marry a cartoon character like me. One element of our life was that Nicole and I never felt we had to discuss or qualify that we were together. It was inherently understood without words that no one outside of what existed between us through Christ's love could interfere. This blessing led to the gift of all gifts, our babies. Jesus gave us a son, Brayden Isaiah, and a daughter, Marlia Grace. I am in tears writing these words. Those children, His children, are the fruit of our sacred union and to the glory of His grace.

None of the above mentioned would or could have ever occurred if I had not turned my life over to Christ. The "old" me would never have understood what it means to be a husband, to honor a covenant relationship, and to sacrifice and give with joy. Gratitude would have been beyond any concept

I could have understood. I would have failed miserably as a father if any element of what was in my life before Jesus was now part of my approach to being a husband and a father. It's not that I never fall short, but because of my spiritual condition and our commitment to the Lord and one another, our little family has been given a blessed home filled with love, light, laughter, and harmony.

I always had a hopeful vision that as a husband and a father I would serve my family well. Fortunately, Nicole and our children have never known me nor seen me as anything other than a sober Christian man. But I've assured my wife often that If she had encountered me before I found the Lord, or worse yet, before I was sober again, she would have sincerely never given me the time of day. This, fortunately, was not His plan. Now we have been together for nearly twelve years, and we are days away from our eleventh wedding anniversary as I write this. We have never looked back. As a father, my children see a godly man who honors their mother and loves them both with every bit of his heart. Our children feel secure knowing their home is built on the foundation of Christ's love. In this, my heart's greatest desires have been given to me.

Every day I strive to be worthy of and to honor the blessing of these sacred people given to me, and I consider it a privilege to provide sacrificially for them. Through the trials and tribulations of my journey, Christ prepared my heart to be a field readied for harvest. The yield it gave under His watchful care has been love and affection. The abundance of love and the gratitude He has given me following my escape from *the void* is best served in being able to shower love on the ones who matter most, my precious family.

Rays of Light—My Precious Gifts:

Never take for granted the blessing of the union in your marriage.

We live in a watching world, so live through attraction, not self-promotion.

Christ must come first. Those you hold the closest benefit from the relationship with your Lord and Savior.

My Heavenly Father wants me to be a father who models His grace, His requirement for biblical obedience, and His infinite love.

Gratitude and daily reminders to not take for granted what has been given to me are critical.

Men, love your wives as Christ loved the church and gave Himself as a sacrifice for her good.

Let your children and family know daily how much you love them through actions and words and make them confident you will never leave.

Put Christ first so you can love your family best. Pour into those who matter most, one day at a time.

He loves us.

He knows us.

He wants a relationship with us all.

He is Lord... our Father... our Savior... our Messiah.

STUDY 9:
MY PRECIOUS GIFTS

Introduction:

I have found day in and day out that I am not my past, nor am I a dictator of my tomorrow. Those words have a remarkable and fascinating list of meanings beyond my understanding, but are relevant to what I'm doing right now. Each trial and tribulation I face has a purpose and a place. I do my work diligently with gratitude and work feverishly on the elimination of resentment.

My greatest and precious gifts I received were not only designed and provided to me, they were also for all the people in my life. This includes all the people who have hurt me. You see, I was, not only transformed, but I am taking a new approach in how life moves forward with most of the same people from the past. My destruction has led me to lead my family into peace. I see this as a precious gift. In this session, I will share how this all unfolded and how my perfect-picture of recovery talked about in Study 4 wasn't even close to the beauty and riches I received. This is where you are heading, and God will restore you better than you were and better than you expected. He has more for you than you can ever imagine.

Wow! Isn't that precious?

Any expectations of what you think life will be like to be recovered—it will all fall short of what you think. The beauty of this fact is that releasing expectations is a tremendous key to propelling us into action. The end result is not what we are working toward or for. The steps, the discovery, the growth, and the peace eclipse the expectations of how it all turns out.

In recovery, one facet of recover I share often is "The only thing that must change is everything." This falls in line with the work we are doing here collectively.

Every area of our lives is often affected by the behavior or habit we are using to fill *the void*. Expect the unexpected and realize the chain reaction that lies ahead. The daily activities you know and love will change. Relationships with family, your personal outlook, your job, and your friends will be transformed through Christ.

Your purpose and ability to be intentional and your approach to objectives will take a radical shift. You will see clearly in ways you had not imagined—how many things you were doing were somehow keeping you from truly dominating and soaring to heights you only dared to dream. Continue to give yourself grace. We are never ready until we are ready. It always takes what it takes to see real change happen. The Lord's timing for us and through us is always His perfect timing.

I've made a commitment—every journey begins with a single step. Please realize as you have prescribed to this journey this is very much a marathon, not a sprint. It is okay to take the time to revel and rejoice in the willingness to be willing. It's a process, and it began when you decided to take that first step.

Safeguard your progress and gains like you would a small child. There will always be areas of progression, but there will also likely be areas of regression. It's okay. We are seeking progress, not perfection. The desire to go to any length to ensure we don't "lose" what we have been given is simple. The work yields results, and the results honor the Lord. This improves ourselves and those we love. So we must take care of this precious gift. This is why I guard this resolve—because I won't want this gift to be taken away. It's precious to me. No voices of discouragement or attack from the enemy will be allowed on my watch.

Much of what I deemed permissible and many of the people I cared for changed when I did. An age-old saying in recovery is "different playgrounds and different playmates." We are re-calibrating our foundation and the essence of who we are. In turn, there is often a chain reaction where things will be different. This is expected and often necessary. This also is a very valid area to pray about as the Lord will guide you to what's ultimately best. I encourage you to pray for your current value system to be increased.

Intentional prayer and living will permeate any and every relationship. The effects will be both large and small. New people will come into your life. Some familiar people will cycle more toward the background, and some unexpected people could resurface. These factors are all part of this journey. Have no fear, and do not hesitate. You are not in this alone. People, places, and things become remarkable and poignant ingredients in the recipe of this dish called life.

Encouragement and Wisdom:

"Therefore everyone who hears these words of mine and puts them into practice is like a wise man who built his house on the rock. The rain came down, the streams rose, and the winds blew and beat against that house; yet it did not fall, because it had its foundation on the rock. But everyone who hears these words of mine and does not put them into practice is like a foolish man who built his house on sand. The rain came down, the streams rose, and the winds blew and beat against that house, and it fell with a great crash." Matthew 7: 24-27

"*Nevertheless, God's solid foundation stands firm, sealed with this inscription: "The Lord knows those who are his," and, "Everyone who confesses the name of the Lord must turn away from wickedness."* 2 Timothy 2:19"

"*For I know the plans I have for you," declares the Lord, "plans to prosper you and not to harm you, to give you hope and a future."* Jeremiah 29:11"

Last Step: Let's reflect.

Put others first moment by moment and day by day. Pour into yourself by giving to others. In prayer, pray intentionally for the men and women who still suffer like you did. Pray to be Christ's instrument and to serve Him best by serving others with kindness and humility. Pray for those you love and those you know. Pray for families and people you don't know. Pray for our country and our leaders. A great thing to remember is that praying for others is a remarkable way to pray for yourself.

My note of encouragement to you:

All of this may seem like a tall order. With what may feel like so many terms and conditions, you may wonder how you will ever manage it all. How will you ever get it all done, much less done correctly? Here's what I have learned: stop, slow down, and take one step at a time. Back and forth, piece by piece, things will be reviewed and put in their rightful place and in their right order. Stay focused on what you've learned. Use best practices and purposefully stay on track. It is better that you took one good step than no step at all. Some elements will become permanent fixtures in your life. You will learn to live by them as naturally as you breathe. Other areas will be on an as-needed basis. Do not give up on where you are headed. Be patient in the journey and take each step forward to your mountaintop.

CHAPTER 10
TRANSFORMATION

"Fear of people and of economic insecurity will leave us."
Alcoholics Anonymous: The Promises #10

When I turned my life over to my Lord and Savior, the only thing that changed for me was everything. But before I explain any more of the amazing changes that God made happen in my life, I feel compelled to make a very basic disclaimer that is authentic and transparent:

I fall short daily.

I have moments where I feel extremely frustrated and show no grace. I'm not proud of these moments. However, I feel convicted in my heart to share those realities, as I know I am the Lord's work in progress. I'm broken and a sinner. I would never want to talk in such a way that my "halo" should blind you.

That being said, by the working of His power in me, my heart, my thoughts, and my outlook have never been the same since I met Christ. Very early in my walk, I noticed that coupled with a deep well of gratitude, I had gained a profound concern for others. The miracle here is that those elements were beyond absent as I headed into my relapses and in the throes of my disease. There have been times along the way where the Holy Spirit has touched me in such a way all I could do is shed tears. Surprisingly, these moments aren't always necessarily profound, nor do they always involve those I love most. Many times, during a simple activity such as taking a walk, a well of gratitude will take shape, and a waterfall of tears will follow. Sometimes, simple reflections or a contemplative moment regarding dear friends I love will a trigger an avalanche of gratitude and emotion. All of these times, and others where pure joy and laughter come into play, are tremendous pieces of the liberation that Jesus Christ has provided for me. I cry tears of joy for the gift of this life, for awareness and a heart to love others, as well as for an impenetrable faith that Christ loves me and spared my life for the glory of His kingdom.

When left to my own devices, I've always been inherently selfish. One of the greatest areas in my life where Christ's presence has made a tremendous impact is in the ability He has given me to love unselfishly. Nicole and I love our children and one another beyond words. The people and families who are in this world with us and who come to our home truly are people we will always be there for. We also love our extended family. Specifically, this area has been where my heart has opened to people carrying burdens. For lack of a better term, our families, in some form or fashion like all the rest of the people in this world, are broken. I understand what they feel, and I trust that what comes to me when I counsel or am confided in is in harmony with God's own heart. This truly is a gift I never take for granted.

Jesus has given me a keen desire to be vulnerable and to risk rejection without fear in order to reach others in need. This gift of love for me translates greatly into my daily life. Whether it's someone helping me at the grocery store or someone who is working at a restaurant, there's a hunger inside of me to see if there is any way I can help impart to them the gift of gratitude so that they can know their worth in those moments as God does. Christ has also blessed both Nicole and me with the gift of wanting to provide for others. I've found that giving both monetarily and of my time ultimately is almost selfish because they both feel so good. In our union, we want to love others well and provide for them in order to celebrate our blessings appropriately.

Truly, all the above mentioned are line items that were never in my DNA. Christ's presence in my heart and the way the Holy Spirit moves me drives this part of my existence. I feel that in any small way possible there may be a moment in which an act of care or compassion can change someone I encounter. Perhaps these times or encounters which I cherish may become part of that individual's foundation where their relationship with Jesus is concerned. These qualities and inherent traits are nothing I can take credit for. The blessing of being able to be there with and for others is a gift that Christ has imparted in me. People have taken a moment to thank me, acknowledge me, or share with me that what was given has had a profound effect on them or their family. During these times, there is a consistent and authentic way I always respond: "I'm an average man, but I serve a great God." I praise the Lord for the gift of these moments with people, and the way He has called Nicole and me to serve others.

Rays of Light—Transformation:

Some of the greatest pleasures are in the smallest moments.

Joy and gratitude are available when we put others first.

Frustration and volatility will come. This is the time to pray.

The Holy Spirit will help us see, hear, love, and live like never before.

STUDY 10: TRANSFORMATION

Introduction:

Growth and perseverance are gifts, true liberations directly dealt from our Heavenly Father. As with any gift or precious thing, it requires and deserves great care. To ensure we do not take for granted what we have been so freely given, we must safeguard the progress by taking care of ourselves. This is not a burden, nor will it be cumbersome. These intentional acts are a privilege and a blessing. These actions and acts proclaim boldly to those around us that we'll do the footwork and are fueled by possibility.

In Study 7, I encouraged you to read Acts 9 regarding the transformation of Saul to Paul. This type of transformation that happens when we ask Jesus into our heart and have God be the Lord of our lives ushers in change only God can bring to remove our pasts and truly transform us.

Through your transformation, there are seven areas in which I want you to give yourself grace and strength to succeed:

1. GRACE - We can strive for perfection, but we need to give ourselves the grace to fall short. We will fall short, we will make mistakes. This is part of the blessing of being focused continuously on making our best better. Those times are gifts, not liabilities, and we never throw the baby out with the bath water.

2. SELFLESSNESS - Put others first in our lives. Intentional action and consideration are wonderful tools. They belong to us now and will serve to help us love others better. We will give back to ourselves by taking care of those around us. This all builds from the inside out. These facts will permeate through many people, especially those closest to us. Even strangers will benefit from this state we remain in.

3. AWARENESS - Be deeply aware of and concerned for others. Think through how any situation could and would affect you. Do this because you want to be mindful of how it affects all those around you. Take the extra time to recognize what is happening around you, and this will impact your life and the ones you love.

4. INSPIRATION - There's a book I love, *A New Pair of Glasses*. It's a perfect title when things just start to look different. We will be awakened to a new way of living, thinking, and loving. Tears of joy, sorrow, and lots of laughter come with the territory. I will simply and comprehensively say any expectation or hope you may have for how life would be will be nothing compared to what I have experienced for myself and the way the Lord has blessed me in my life.

5. COURAGE - You have broken the chain of dysfunction. You're now the leader of your family—you're the catalyst for your family's future. The old tapes, the old patterns, and the history that had defined you literally carry no weight.

6. RESOLVE - We are not victims, but victors. We will fall rank and file to our rightful positions, front and center. This is not an easy task, nor one we will always want the responsibility of. At the end of the day, it's an inevitable part of stepping away from the hurt. We have, with God's care and love, created a new normal. In the land of the blind, the one-eyed man leads… on we go front and center.

7. SERVANTHOOD - Your growth, journey, trials, and tribulations will help serve others every day. Some of the smallest acts or actions which seem mundane and inconsequential to you may be a tipping point for someone you encounter. As the days go by and you continue to grow, you will quickly realize the effect you have on others. Some of your greatest challenges are serving others to a degree you never considered.

Encouragement and Wisdom:

Re-read Acts 9:1-19.

"Look at the birds of the air; they do not sow or reap or store away in barns, and yet your heavenly Father feeds them. Are you not much more valuable than they?" Matthew 6:26

"Your word is a lamp for my feet, a light on my path." Psalm 119:105

Last Step: Let's reflect.

There are so many analogies that come to mind as I offer you a summary of all that's available. Tools in a toolbox, paints on a pallet, channels on a cable system (almost too many), but you get the point. The true gift is in that it always has been there for you.

As our eyes open and we experience life, we realize how much we need daily prayer. We are now gaining a group of new contemporaries who are like-minded and participants in healthy lifestyles who surround us. There is music, specifically worship music, filled with messages of hope and harmony that will suddenly ring true in a way they never have before.

There is the Holy Spirit, our Lord and Savior. Christ will continue to fill your heart and will allow you the joy of having it overflow. This, and everything that goes along with it all, is now officially yours. Again, they were always there. But it takes your willingness to see through the work you're doing that will provide access and inspiration again and again in your days ahead.

My note of encouragement to you:

You are worth it—all of it. You are loved, and you have been chosen. Trust that and know that this infinite truth is the prescriber of your life. Despair and regret will remain where they belong in the rearview mirror. Hope, gratitude, and glory will become the tapestry of this rich and rewarding time for you. This critical point is your foundation and will be built upon. We never leave before the miracle, and we all continue to live knowing the best is yet to come.

CHAPTER 11
THE DAILY GIFT
I GIVE MYSELF

"That feeling of uselessness and self-pity will disappear."
Alcoholics Anonymous: The Promises #6[xvii]

As I live this life in union with God, the indication of how it goes and how I live up to what has been so graciously bestowed upon me always depends upon my spiritual condition. Many critical factors will define that condition—most notably, the overall state of my self-care and self-love. There are many actions and conditions that define what this looks like at any given time, but I have found that the recipe I need in order to live by the power that Christ is ready to give me each day includes the following ingredients:

1. Prayer - The first and greatest indicator of how well I am doing is the condition of my prayer life. It is a non-negotiable foundational piece where my best interest and ability to serve others are concerned. Every morning I must be on my knees, taking the time to reach out to the Lord. I earnestly ask Him to help others in need, taking to Him the elements I'm not able to control where people, places, and things are concerned. One huge need I have in my personal prayer life is to pray for individuals I'm having issues with and/or carrying resentment toward. Bringing these painful things to God can be monumentally challenging, but I absolutely must be on guard for places where I'm carrying resentments, my worst enemy. There is a common saying about resentments I have found personally to be very true: *"Resentment is the act of drinking poison and hoping the other person dies."* Praying ensures I'm not carrying resentments with me daily. In the evening, I hit my knees again to give thanks for another day, to examine what is in my heart, and to revisit anything else that a day in this world might have served up.

2. Exercise - My physical condition also ties in greatly to my spiritual well-being. The gym and areas where I can physically exert myself seem to strengthen my spirit. I go through a tremendous amount of gratitude as it's a reminder that my health, despite my best efforts to destroy myself, was safe-guarded and restored through my Heavenly Father.

3. Diet - The way I'm eating ties into my spiritual condition, as well. I am prone to be someone who will emotionally eat. I have been enlightened knowing that I'm very much a trigger eater. Like in my addiction, I'm similarly an all-

or-nothing person where my nutrition is concerned; I'm either on track and honoring my commitment in that area or I'm a roaming, grazing, buffet hound. I never have understood people who have "a" cookie, and my reaction to cake is an apropos example, too. Don't even get me started on cake. I'm likely to eat myself into the emergency room if the right cake is available (I LOVE CAKE).

4. Surroundings - There are also some geographical, physical places that feed my soul in this life. Church has and continues to be a place where I feel so close to the Holy Spirit and where I feel the brightest places in my heart easily reaching out for Him. I also love the sense of peace and health I feel whenever I have time at the beach. The ocean is so remarkable to me and an incredible illustration of the Lords magnificence. I always find myself emerged in gratitude and blessings when I'm walking outdoors in every and any kind of nature. When I see people interacting in these environments and see the beauty and majesty of the Lord's world, I feel humbled and whole. These physical settings bring are a consistent reminder for me to what matters most and allow me to stay grounded in gratitude.

5. Empathy - Authentic communication and consistent emphasis on putting others first also helps me safe- guard and care for myself and maintain a healthy and whole spiritual condition.

6. Communication - In addition, I find that I need and must share my feelings with those I love. The Lord has instilled in me that I must not take for granted that those I love are always fully aware of it. My heart is convicted to show them and tell them often. I'm extremely grateful for this part of my daily reality as it feels so good and fills up a great deal of the emptiness that ate away at me during my travail in *the void*.

The above are some of my touch points through which I continue to learn and grow. I continue to add and delete items as well, as the Lord keeps working on my heart and opens my mind and my eyes to serve Him best each day.

Rays of Light—The Daily Gift I Give Myself:

Follow the Lord's "recipe" for your life.

Focus on the disciplines, people, and places that strengthen your spirit.

Avoid like the plague the places, things, and people that pull you down.

Love others well, love yourself well, love Christ always, and put Him above everything and everyone.

Speak from your heart and speak truth. Do not hold on to hurt; own it, voice it, and take the power away from it.

Live in an attitude of prayer: prayers of gratitude, prayers for grace, prayers for those who have wronged you, prayers of peace, prayers of thanks, prayers about everything.

Know that you are chosen, loved, and pursued.

STUDY 11:
THE DAILY GIFT
I GIVE MYSELF

(Self-care—it's critical for you.)

Introduction:

I love gift cards, store credits, and gift certificates. LOVE! But none of these mean anything if I don't use them. The same applies to everything we have learned through these studies if we don't apply them. The recipe for what is best for us must be created through what we do each day. We must be vigilante and intentional. It is work to ensure we take the best care of ourselves. Faith without works may very well be dead, but if we will do the work, then we can safeguard all we have to offer to those we love. This fact and these actions continue to allow us to give back and to move forward. Then we can provide in ways we would have never dreamed. We have earned this right, and we will pay the price to reap what we sow.

Main Points to Cover in Study:

It's unselfish to take care of yourself. You need it.

Here are some practical things you can do:

1. Go take a walk.

2. Invest in relationships (throw a ball with your son, tea with your daughter, movie with your wife, shut your phone off at the end of the day).

3. Play games as a family.

4. Bake together.

5. Pour into someone else—it will pour back into you. For example, ask, "Can I make your burden smaller for you?" Or admit, "I can't do it myself, if it's just me I will fail. I need others to be my support system and I want to be theirs."

List out the things you can and will do to give back to yourself:

1._____

2._____

3._____

Encouragement and Wisdom:

"As iron sharpens iron, so one person sharpens another." Proverbs 27:17

"For just as each of us has one body with many members, and these members do not all have the same function, so in Christ we, though many, form one body, and each member belongs to all the others." Romans 12: 4-5

"Now you are the body of Christ, and each one of you is a part of it.." 1 Corinthians 12:27

Last Step: Let's reflect.

None of us are meant to do this alone. I want to encourage you to find a local church. This may take more than one visit to experience the church. You will know, though—you will know as sure as you know your name when you are in the right place for what the Lord wants for you. You will find yourself surrounded and welcomed warmly by like-minded individuals, and you will feel at home.

Churches, like people, are not perfect. Just like those loved ones we hold dear, we will love our church family even through their imperfections. We deserve a safe place to worship, to grow, and to develop relationships.

Once you have settled in at a church, find a way to be of service. Financial support is easy, needed, and appreciated. Finding where you can serve at your church is when you will start making a tremendous impact. Again, this will be an area where you will feel selfish by giving because you will see quickly how much you will get back.

Do not hesitate, nor be afraid, to find your place and plug in. The church is only the church by the sum of its people— meaning that you can find community and connection with other believers in and out of a typical church setting. The main thing I want to encourage you to do is to find a church, a group of believers where you can be supported and serve. You were meant to find a church home. It is a part of the journey and footwork that must happen in order for you to receive the reward of belonging to a loving family and experiencing community.

My note of encouragement to you:

"There's no place like home, there's no place like home…" possibly one of the wisest movie lines ever from the *Wizard of Oz*. Home is many things. Not just that great blessed roof over our heads. Home is community. Home is a small group where a study and fellowship can occur. Home is church. Home is a moment of prayer. These comforts, the safety of these surroundings, and the gifts it all provides come with the territory. So we must make a home. We must be steadfast and decisive; we must take action and execute. It is time to move in and provide ourselves with a proverbial base camp where we can prosper and grow. Again, this may go against the grain of what we deem ourselves worthy of receiving. That false perception is irrelevant. We are worthy and worth it. Our new home is waiting for us, so walk through the doors and be loved.

CHAPTER 12
A PRAYER FOR US ALL

"We will comprehend the word serenity and we will know peace."

Alcoholics Anonymous: The Promises #4[xviii]

I have a consistent hope and vision for the use of these words you have just read. My hope is that, if it is Christ's desire, they will create a platform from which I can share with others the freedom and joy that has been so freely given to me. Also, that someone who has read this, in their time of need or trouble, would remember that what happens for eternity matters most in our lives. I contemplate daily that I, too, must remember this truth to keep me in the healthiest perspective.

Sometimes I lose sight of the gift of His love given for us right here and now when my earthly desires and sins rob me of my confidence toward Him—the most precious truth that I am so convicted to share with others. Despite this, He remains my Heavenly Father, there loving me, encouraging me, and carrying me always in His arms.

I want to give you a prayer, a prayer to be an embodiment of all that you have seen while reading this story of how God loved a sinner like me back into life.

Father I call out to You, reach out to You, implore You on behalf of all those I love and all those You love—help us. Help us, Father, to be rid of petty desires that get in the way of serving You well. Help us, Father, to carry even some degree of grace toward others in the same way You offer infinite grace and love to us. Help us, Father, to open our hearts and be vulnerable, and make ourselves available to others despite our self-centered nature, in the same way You are always available for us. Help us, Father, to live in a manner You deem appropriate in honoring those closest to us and honoring those we come across the way we honor You, and in the way You bless us with your unconditional love and mercy. Help us, Father, to love and live with utter abandonment, void of our own expectations. Let us give first, expect nothing, and find our greatest return in knowing that we are pleasing You. Help us, Father, to be authentic and transparent, to offer our most genuine and best selves out of love for You. Help us stay focused on You for eternity, especially when comparison to one another is robbing us of the joy and blessings of this life and the love You have given us. Help us, Father, moment by moment, and day by day until we are blessed to be in Your kingdom. Please help us to know and live Your truth while we are here. Help us to know as we trudge through our time in this world that this temporary stop is followed by the glory of our eternal life by Your side. Father, we ask all of these things in the name of Your blessed son, Jesus. Amen.

I want to tell you, whoever it is reading this now, whether we are family, friends, acquaintances, or work contemporaries, if we have never met at all or perhaps met in some sort of a wonderful passing moment, I must tell you what I know. I have a God who loves me—a patient, loving, nurturing, and caring Heavenly Father who loves me always—and He loves you, too, in the same way. God bless us all as we take this walk together for the glory of His kingdom.

Always, in His name.

Principals of Filling *the Void*

He is present.

He loves us.

He knows us.

He wants a relationship with us all.

He is Lord, our Father, our Savior, our Messiah.

STUDY 12:
A PRAYER FOR US ALL

My Prayer

Here we are together. Piece-by-piece we have examined and re-examined steps and practices to ensure that the gains and progress are permanent fixtures, not temporary remedies. All this being said, I offer you this prayer. My prayer for you is to honor your remarkable commitment.

Father God, thank you!

Thank you for the desire and the hope to know and live the truth. Help us, Lord, to move forward boldly and to give ourselves grace as you give us grace in each moment of regression.

We love you, Father, and as we persevere, allow us to be open to being transparent and to be willing to step out in faith each day for the reward You have for us. Help us to remain available to ourselves and others through You. Please, Father, continue to help us keep in mind those who need You most just like us. Help us be a living example of Your grace and glory. Help us be present and live through the attraction, not promotion of Your infinite love and care. We love You, Father. You gave us Your son. Help us a day at a time to continue to offer You our hearts.

To all this in thanksgiving we say together, Amen.

Encouragement and Wisdom:

"The greatest among you will be your servant." Matthew 23:11

"And do not forget to do good and to share with others, for with such sacrifices God is pleased." Hebrews 13:16

"A new command I give you: Love one another. As I have loved you, so you must love one another." John 13:34

"Jesus replied: 'Love the Lord your God with all your heart and with all your soul and with all your mind.' This is the first and greatest commandment. And the second is like it: 'Love your neighbor as yourself.'" Matthew 22:37-39

My note of encouragement to you:

I am honored, humbled, and awestruck by what you have given me. You have given me time from your life—time you will never get back, but time I earnestly pray will create a return for you and for those you love. I am in no position to ask you for anything after this remarkable gift you have bestowed upon me. I am not worthy of it, but I serve a God who sought for me to do this work. Amidst all of this adulation I ask you to share how this work has been a benefit to you. Please email me or leave direct feedback on our website. If there is an area of need, let me know. If you have a question, let me know. If you need additional help more than what is in this book, then please email me as well. You are worth it, there is more to build on, and it's okay!

Do not deny yourself the benefit of reaching out and getting the help you need. We are not alone. We are in this together, and we never need to hesitate where reaching out for one another is concerned. We are family, united by the fabric and DNA of our Lord and Savior Jesus Christ—blessed and honored as a family in our Father.

On we go, together trudging this road of happy destiny.

Welcome to the family!

ABOUT THE AUTHOR

Steven Ginsburg is a follower of Jesus. A husband and a father. A sober addict and alcoholic, saved and spared by the grace of God.

With a professional career spanning thirty plus years in commercial real estate, he focused most on the time-share industry. As one of the two founding partners and principals of Restore Detox Centers in Poway, California, and the facility's chief executive officer, Steven's life turned full time toward work in recovery. His commitment to helping others overcome addictions also drove the creation of CurePro, a support-based professional services organization that provides information and solutions for the pandemic of drug and alcohol perils.

Steven was born and raised in Highland Park, Illinois, and currently resides in North County San Diego, California.

His passion and conviction continue to carry him a day at a time to serve others in their times of crisis. He conveys with conviction and living assurance through Christ's grace and mercy that there is a solution to overcoming a life of hopelessness, driven by addictions.

Please visit www.curepro.com to learn more about CurePro and Steven's work. Steven can be contacted directly by email at steven@curepro.com.

Endnotes

i. "Data on Excessive Drinking," Centers for Disease Control and Prevention, accessed July 31, 2020, https://www.cdc.gov/alcohol/data-stats.html.

ii. "Drug Overdose Deaths," Centers for Disease Control and Prevention, accessed July 31, 2020, https://www.cdc.gov/drugoverdose/data/statedeaths.html.

iv. AA Promise #12

v. "Celebrities Who Are Open About Addiction," WebMD, reviewed October 8, 2018, https://www.webmd.com/mental-health/addiction/ss/slideshow-celebs-addiction-recovery.

vi. AA Promise #3

vii. AA Promise #2

viii. AA Promise #1

ix. AA Promise #8

x. AA Promises - © Alcoholics Anonymous 4th Edition, page # 83-84

xi. AA Promise #5

xii. AA Promise #11

xiii. AA Promise #9

xiv. There are many rephrases and variants of this quote, but the original is attributed to Spanish philosopher, essayist, poet, and novelist George Santayana (1863-1952), who wrote in *The Life of Reason: The Phases of Human Progress* (1905-1906), "Those who cannot remember the past are condemned to repeat it."

xv. AA Promise #7

xvi. A New Pair of Glasses by Charles A. Chamberlain, New-Look Publishing Company

xvii. AA Promise #6

xviii. AA Promise #4

Join our tribe at www.wholy-living.com

NOTES